EARLY WAR PHOTOGRAPHS

Frontispiece
Encampment of the Army of the Potomac, May–June 1862
Photograph by James F. Gibson   Copyright: Library of Congress, Washington DC

EARLY WAR PHOTOGRAPHS

Compiled and written by

PAT HODGSON

Osprey

Published in 1974 by
Osprey Publishing Ltd., 137 Southampton Street,
Reading Berkshire.

Designed by Behram Kapadia.

Filmset and printed by BAS Printers Limited,
Wallop, Hampshire.

Contents

Indian Mutiny 1857–9

Chinese Wars 1856–60

American Civil War 1861–5

Japan 1864

Tibet 1904

Index

Introduction

The second half of the nineteenth century saw the beginning of the whole modern movement in mass communications. For centuries the battles and human suffering caused by war could only be viewed second-hand, as recreated by the artist. With the discovery of photography for the first time the ordinary soldiers and the mud of the battlefield could be shown. There was an authenticity to a photograph which convinced people that here was reality at last. It was much later that a greater sophistication showed that something which was apparently first-hand evidence could be just as biased as an artist's impression. It is difficult for us today to understand the impact that these first photographs made. Their veracity was never doubted. Here was a moment in time forever frozen. At the same time as the photographers, the first war correspondents and pictorial journalists arrived on the scene. These men became a familiar sight with the forces from the 1850s onwards, and they were kept busy, as there was not a year throughout the period when there was no fighting somewhere.

Inevitably, it was first thought that photography would be possible during battle. The apochryphal young lady in *Punch* expressed what was probably in the minds of the first photographers when she wrote to her fiancé in the Crimea saying: 'I send you, dear Alfred, a complete photographic apparatus which will amuse you doubtless in your moments of leisure, and if you could send me home, dear, a good view of a nice battle, I should feel extremely obliged. PS. If you could take the view, dear, just in the moment of victory, I should like it all the better.' In fact, this cosy attitude to fighting was not quite so outlandish as it sounds today. During the Crimean War civilians and relations did watch battles from a safe distance, although the primitive cameras in use would have made it quite impossible to take any clear photograph of the action. Gentlemen making a 'Grand Tour' of Europe often took in the battlefields at the same time, and one of these, 'J L', wrote to the *Photographic News* in 1859 saying: 'When I left England my intention was to make a tour with the camera to Switzerland, but the exciting prospect of being able to get plates of battle-fields, sieges, and other incidental scenes, made me change my course' – in this case for Italy and the war with Austria. 'JL' was among the first of the freelance war photographers, but none of his photographs have survived. This somewhat detached view of war was also to change during the latter part of the nineteenth century. With increasing industrialization and new weapons, it became difficult to isolate fighting to a small area, and modern total war involving the whole population began to be inevitable. Photography was a technical process which was particularly suitable to depict the ever-increasing technicalities of war.

When an artist's impression was all that was available, and there was no illustrated Press, the number of people who could see war pictures was limited. Painters developed a heroic style which was anything but realistic, but appealed to the prosperous classes. Photography was a democratic art, as many copies of a print could be circulated, and this meant that ordinary people could see for the first time what war was like. It was quickly discovered that it was not technically possible to photograph the heroic battle scenes beloved by painters, and the photographer had to search for other means of expression. Until the end of the century war photographers had to make a static scene significant. They were restricted to single or group portraits, ruined buildings, deserted battlefields and dead bodies, and interpreted these in their different ways. Some, like Roger Fenton, had a painter's approach and posed their characters to tell a story. Felice Beato, on the other hand, tried to find significant form in ruined buildings and destroyed forts, and his photographs are a complex pattern of textures and shapes. Artists were wary of competition from photographers and certainly portrait photography deprived them of a lot of work. But the traffic between art and photography was not only one-way. Painters found that they could copy from photographs, and the *Art Journal* of 1856 describes two paintings based on a Roger Fenton photograph of the Crimea. Both artists, Augustus Egg and R. Jones Barker, had copied Fenton's photograph of the Allied generals in consultation with Omar Pasha before Sebastopol. The artists employed by the illustrated journals also frequently used photographs for reference, their drawings thus depending even less on direct observation. The photographers in the field were often scornful of the war artist's attempts. Fenton, for instance, criticizes Edward Goodhall of the *Illustrated London News* for his drawings of the Crimea: 'His sketches which appear in the paper seem to astonish everyone from their total want of likeness to the reality.' At the end of the century painters of battle scenes suffered another blow from photography when Eadweard Muybridge proved that one of their great strengths, the depiction of the movement of horses, was based on a misconception.

Very few of the numerous war photographs taken in the nineteenth century have survived. It was a disposable art in the days before half-tone reproduction was possible. For each exposure made there was a negative and a handful of prints. The majority of negatives taken during the period were glass and were easily broken. Many deteriorated in bad storage conditions until the whole surface started to peel off. The prints soon became crumpled and torn, and inadequate fixing methods meant that others faded. Usually it was the photographs mounted in albums which were preserved, as they were less exposed to light and damage. There were some unsuccessful attempts to use photographs for book illustration, and on occasion actual photographic prints were pasted into the book, a very expensive and time-consuming process which was used for Alexander Gardner's *Photographic Sketch Book of the Civil War*. The only way of reproducing a photograph in the Press during most of the period was in the form of a drawing printed as a wood-engraving. Actual photographs could not be reproduced until the invention of the half-tone block in 1880, and the first picture reproduced by this means appeared in the *Daily Graphic*, New York, on 4 March 1880. In 1884 the *Photographic News* commented: 'Not only is the engraved block made entirely by photographic agency, but it represents current news, and what is perhaps of more importance, it was printed satisfactorily along with the rapidly machined letterpress.' By the 1890s the illustrated journals were all using photographs, but newspapers did not follow suit for many years.

The first examples of war photography occur very early in photographic history, and are interesting for the techniques used rather than for the content of the pictures. Some daguerreotypes made during the Mexican War (1846–8) are generally considered to be the first war photographs. The daguerreotype method was first made public in 1839 and continued to be used side by side with other techniques until the early 1850s. The pictures were taken on copper which had been plated with a thin layer of silver and needed an exposure of about five minutes. Each picture was an original, as there was no negative. The process was more suitable for portraiture, and the Mexican War photographs were probably taken by a local daguerreotypist in Saltillo, Mexico, who normally specialized in portraits. John MacCosh, whose album of calotypes is in the National Army Museum, London, has an equal claim to being one of the earliest war photographers. He was the first in the tradition of the soldier who was also an amateur photographer. MacCosh was a surgeon with the Bengal Infantry, and during the 2nd Sikh War (1848–9) took portraits of his fellow officers and of the commanders, Lord Gough and Sir Charles Napier. The calotype process which he used had only been patented by Fox Talbot in 1841, and would still not have been easily available to amateurs. The negative was made on sensitized paper, and the time of exposure varied between three and five minutes, which meant that the photographer was restricted to portraits and architecture. The detail of the prints was poor in comparison with a daguerreotype, but it was a comparatively cheap and simple method, and pictures as large as 12″ × 16″ could be produced. Being a negative process, more than one copy could also be made. MacCosh was also present at the 2nd Burma War (1852–3), and extended his range to include captured cities with troops and equipment in the foreground.

The Crimean War set the pattern for war reporting which was to go on until the end of the century. For the first time photographers, correspondents and artists from all countries were on campaign. The new illustrated journals had started shortly before and there was a demand for verbal and pictorial news. The face of war was also changing. British Army organization had not altered much since Waterloo, but railways were now used to move supplies and troops, messages could be passed by telegraphy, and field kitchens and an efficient nursing service were being organized for the first time. William Howard Russell was reporting the campaign on behalf of *The Times*, and in 1854 it was suggested in Britain that 'accurate representations of the realities of war and its contingent scenery' might be made by photography.[1] The Government decided to send out a small photographic unit in March 1854 under Captain John Hackett of the 77th (East Middlesex) Regiment. A civilian photographer, Roger Nicklin of Manchester, was appointed, and they left for Varna with sixteen boxes of equipment in the transport ship, *Rip Van Winkle*. Unhappily, the ship and photographers were lost during a hurricane off Balaclava in November 1854. Russell described the scene a few days earlier when the sea 'rushed up the precipices in masses of water and foam, astonishing by their force and fury'.[2] In the same year a Rumanian photographer, Carol Popp de Szathmari, made his way independently to the Crimea. He was a man of some renown, and was court painter and photographer to one of the Rumanian dukes, with a good deal of experience and powerful patrons. It is ironic that all his photographs have been lost, although at the time his prints were much admired, and he presented copies of his albums to Queen Victoria, the French Emperor Napoleon III and to Franz Joseph of Austria. One album was exhibited at the Universal Exhibition of 1855 in Paris. A description of his work has been left by Ernest Lacan in *Esquisses photographiques, apropos de l'exposition universelle et de la guerre d'orient*, showing that he covered much of the same ground as Roger Fenton, who arrived in the Crimea a year later, but he did have one advantage, which was that he had access to the Russian and Turkish lines. By a chance of history, Fenton has been given the place of the first great war photographer.

Roger Fenton was a painter by early training and had been interested in photography for some years, founding the Photographic Society of London in 1853. He arrived in the Crimea in February 1855 with the intention of taking photographs privately. He was fortunate in having influential friends – in particular, the Queen and Prince Albert – who smoothed the way for him and made it easier for him to live in reasonable comfort on campaign. He was financed by a Manchester publisher, Thomas Agnew, who was intending to sell the photographs commercially. Fenton's instinctive feeling for composition and atmosphere made his photographs an immediate success with his Victorian audience. His carefully posed groups of people look remarkably natural considering the fact that they had to stay still for at least fifteen seconds while the photograph was taken. Fenton left a very full account of his four months in the Crimea, reported in the *Journal of the Photographic Society* in January 1856. He used the wet collodion process of photography, the details of which were first made public by Frederick Scott Archer in 1851. The process continued to be used up to 1880, although a dry-plate method had been experimented with long before this. Wet-plate photography, using a glass plate, which was manipulated throughout in a wet condition, was a cumbersome business. This meant that a portable dark-room had to accompany the photographer wherever he went, as the plate had to be first dipped in a sensitizing bath, exposed in the camera while still wet and then taken out and developed. Fenton records that he took a stock of 700 glass plates with him, 'fitted into grooved boxes, each of which contained about 24 plates; the boxes of glass were again packed in chests, so as to insure their security'.[3] The camera he used was bulky and heavy and needed to be mounted on a solid wood tripod. As a portable dark-room, he converted a van, which would also be a place in which to live, eat and sleep. Fenton took the photographs, but had with him two assistants, William the handyman and cook, and Marcus Sparling, a former corporal in the 4th Light Dragoons, as driver and to look after the horses. The assistants also lent a hand with the printing. The van was under fire on several occasions and became hot and uncomfortable when the summer came. Fenton said: 'As soon as the van door was closed to commence the preparation of the plate perspiration started from every pore, and the sense of relief was great when it was possible to open the door to breathe even the hot air outside. . . . One drinks like a fish. I reckoned yesterday that I took seventeen tumblers of liquid, nine of which were tea, two champagne and the rest beer.' By June it was impossible to work after 10 a.m. and a heat haze obscures the background in some of the photographs. The chemicals were also affected. The collodion poured on to the glass plate sometimes dried before it was spread evenly and it was difficult to keep the silver nitrate bath used to sensitize the plates at the right temperature. Dust and flies added to the problems. Fenton's van was a centre of interest among the troops, and he recalls that he was constantly in demand to take portraits, 'and if I refuse to take them, I get no facilities for conveying my van from one locality to another'. When the time came to return to England there was the problem of transporting the glass plates safely. In a letter written in June 1855 Fenton says: 'I shall bring the negatives with me, as it would not be safe to send them, and to get them home uninjured, even with my own supervision, will cause much trouble unless I am lucky enough to get them shipped in a vessel going straight to England.'[4] On his return to England his photographs were exhibited at the Gallery of the Water Colour Society in Pall Mall, and later all over the country. They were much admired, and Thomas Agnew must have been pleased with his investment.

For the next few years all war photographers had similar problems to those encountered by Fenton. Others at the Crimea whose prints have survived were Jean Charles Langlois, a French Army officer, and two gifted amateur photographers, James Robertson and Felice Beato, who arrived in the Crimea about the time that Fenton left for England. Robertson was chief engraver to the Imperial Mint at Constantinople, and up to the time of the Crimean War had been engaged in taking views of exotic cities with Beato. Robertson's camp scenes and panoramic views are straightforward, honest photographs, with none of the theatrical quality which is so compelling in Fenton's work. Beato, an Italian by birth, was particularly interested in architectural photography at this time, a fact which was reflected in his war pictures. After the war both continued to produce sets of Mediterranean views, and were in India in 1857 to record the Mutiny. Beato was commissioned by the War Department to take documentary photographs of the destruction of the buildings at Lucknow. To do this he used a camera with large 10″ × 12″ plates, which needed a long exposure, but gave prints with a good detail and a subtle gradation of tone. He did what was required of him by the War Department, but his beautifully composed photographs completely transcend the world of record photography. While in India he also took portraits of Army officers, of local people and of any building that caught his interest. After the Mutiny Robertson remained in India to work with the old-established firm of Shepherd of Simla. Beato went on to China and took equally meticulous photographs of the interior of the Taku forts and the corpses of the defenders. Later he was one of the first European photographers in Japan, taking one of his first action shots showing a French landing force at Akama Fort in 1864. His main interest was never war photography, but he had very much more experience than anyone else during the early period, and was even in Egypt in 1884–5 to cover part of the Sudan campaign.

War photography came of age with the American Civil War, and the man responsible for a sizeable part of the photographic activity on the Union side was Matthew Brady. Brady's purpose was to record the war for historical reasons as much as for commercial ones, and there is an honesty of approach characteristic of everything taken by his team of photographers. Style does not get in the way of content, and these pictures have much more in common with the Press photographs of the present century than with Beato's Chinese pictures taken only a year earlier. Brady was a fashionable portrait photographer and interested in photography as a means of recording social history. In 1845 he had started on a collection of portraits of 'Illustrious Americans', using the daguerreotype process. When war broke out he had a lucrative business, with galleries in New York and Washington and a team of photographers which included Alexander Gardner. Knowing so many important members of the Government through his photographic business, he soon got permission to go to the front, but he had to provide the funds for the expedition himself. He equipped a photographic wagon, similar to Fenton's, which soon became known as the 'What-is-it Wagon' among the Army of the Potomac. Brady became famous at the 1st Battle of Bull Run in July 1861, when he took a number of photographs and came under fire. His wagon was overturned, but he managed to rescue some of his glass plates. *Humphrey's Journal* suspected that the enemy thought his camera was a 'great steam gun discharging 500 balls a minute, and immediately took to their heels when they got within its focus'.[5] The *Journal's* correspondent was full of enthusiasm for Brady's photographs, saying: 'His are the only reliable records at Bull Run. . . . Brady never misrepresents.' William Russell of *The Times*, on the other hand, came in for some criticism for his misleading reports: 'the man who was celebrated for writing graphic letters when there was nobody to contradict him, but who had proved, by his correspondence from his country, that but little confidence can be placed in his accounts. See him as he flies for dear life, with his notes sticking out of his pockets'. After his spectacular start, Brady realized that he would not be able to cover personally all the fronts in the war as well as continue to manage his fashionable galleries in New York and Washington. He organized the work on mass-production lines, sending out a team of photographers into the field and arranging for the negatives to be printed by Anthony & Co. At one time he was said to have had twenty photographers on campaign. 'I had men in all parts of the army,' said Brady, 'like a rich newspaper.'[6] Since he financed and employed the photographers, Brady was not scrupulous about giving credits for the pictures they took, and everything went out under his own name. This later led to trouble. Now many of the photographs once credited to Brady have been found to have been taken by someone else, and the pendulum has swung so far the other way that it is difficult to prove that any war photograph was actually taken by Brady himself.

The star of Brady's photographic team was Alexander Gardner, a Scot, who had been in charge of Brady's Washington gallery since 1858. Gardner was an interesting character whose fare to America had been paid by Brady in 1856, presumably on account of his photographic ability. He was a cultured man, interested in astronomy, optics and chemistry, and was also efficient on the administrative side of running Brady's photographic business. Gardner was attached to the Army of the Potomac under General McClellan early in 1862 as a civilian, with the rank of Captain. He was responsible for the usual Army photographic jobs of copying maps and plans, but he was also able to take numerous views of the battlefields of McClellan's Peninsular Campaign. After McClellan was relieved of his command Gardner returned to Washington, broke with Brady and set up his own rival gallery. This may have been caused by Brady's unwillingness to acknowledge his photographers by name or by the Brady studio's financial difficulties. At any rate, Gardner was always very careful to credit his own photographic team, many of whom were ex-employees of Brady. He had a pressman's sense of news and was present at many important occasions neglected by Brady, including the execution of the Lincoln conspirators in July 1865. In 1866 he published a *Photographic Sketch Book of the War*, containing 100 original prints, each with a rather partisan description, and with the date and photographer's name carefully recorded. In 1869 he tried unsuccessfully to get Congress to purchase his war photographs, saying: 'In procuring the above views, the undersigned devoted much time, great labor, and considerable expense. He has always regarded them as having a National character and has long indulged the hope that they would some day belong to the Nation. They are beyond the reach of private enterprise in both their value and importance.'[7] Congress was unimpressed. By 1867 he had closed his gallery and become a field photographer for the Union Pacific Railroad.

Timothy O'Sullivan was another gifted photographer who started work with Brady, but later went over to Gardner and stayed with him for seven years. One of the most haunting photographs of the war, 'The Harvest of Death', was taken by O'Sullivan on the battlefield of Gettysburg. After the war O'Sullivan, like Gardner, had developed a taste for travel and became a photographer for government geological surveys and expeditions. The Union side had far better photographic coverage than the Confederates. Brady and Gardner had working for them at different times O'Sullivan, Alexander Gardner's brother James, David Knox, J.F. Coonley, T.C. Roche, J. Reekie and many others. Roche, who later transferred to the Anthony studio to take stereoscopic views, had some narrow escapes before Petersburg in 1865. There were also the photographers who had Army appointments, whose chief work was to copy plans and to do minor secret service work. These included George Barnard, Sam Cooley and Captain A.T. Russell. Russell's work was largely confined to views of railway systems. Samuel Cooley was attached to the 10th Corps and took pictures of Jacksonville, St Augustine, Beaufort and Charleston during the bombardment. Barnard was with Sherman on his march to the sea and published a collection of photographs taken then. The Engineer Corps had photographs taken of installations of particular interest in the engineering field.

The Confederate side lacked a Brady to co-ordinate photographic documentation of the war, but every town had its own photographer. The most well known were George Cook of Charleston and A.D. Lytle of Baton Rouge. Cook, who in pre-war days had worked for Brady, took an interesting photograph of ironclads in action in September 1863, when the ships *Weehawken*, *Montauk* and *Passaic* fired on Confederate batteries at Fort Moultrie. 'Although Fort Moultrie was the aim of their gunners, Cook, with his head under the dark cloth, saw on the ground-glass a shell passing within a few feet of him. Another shell knocked one of his plate holders off the parapet into the rain water cistern. He gave a soldier five dollars to fish it out for him.'[8] Unfortunately, this photograph, taken in such dramatic circumstances, has not survived. Lytle had the hazardous job of 'Camera spy' for the Confederate Secret Service and was detailed to take pictures of Federal batteries, gunboats, cavalry and anything of strategical interest. Confederate photographers were at a disadvantage compared with their Union opposite numbers, because Anthony & Co. of New York were the main suppliers of photographic chemicals, and the South had to smuggle theirs through the blockade masquerading as quinine, which was allowed in as 'medical goods'.

Wet-plate photography as described by Fenton was generally in use throughout the Civil War, though daguerreotypes and tintypes were also sometimes made for portraits. There was a boom in portrait photography caused by the war, keeping small-town photographers who were not at the front busy in their studios and at military camps. 'A camp is hardly pitched before one of the omnipresent artists in collodion and amber-varnish drives up his two-horse wagon, pitches his canvas gallery, and unpacks his chemicals.' The Bergstresser brothers from Pennsylvania took in one day 160 portraits at $1.00 each and 'if anybody knows an easier and better way of making money than that, the public should know it', wrote the correspondent of the *New York Tribune* in 1862.[9] Although many of the photographs taken at the Civil War have long since been destroyed, countless portraits of soldiers remain in family archives, and Miller's *Photographic History of the Civil War*, printed in 1912, has preserved some of the others before the originals were lost. Most war photographers carried stereoscopic as well as large-plate cameras, because they hoped to sell large quantities of these more cheaply produced prints. Stereoscopic photography, which involved similar developing processes to those used for large-plate cameras, was popular from the 1850s until the end of the century. Two almost identical photographs were taken and mounted side by side, and when seen through a viewer a three-dimensional effect was obtained. Brady, whose vision and energy had been responsible for a large part of the war photography, got little financial reward. The value of his prints was reduced, as he had given Anthony & Co. a duplicate set of his negatives. Public interest in the war had waned, the Government would not buy his negatives for the nation, and he was at last forced to sell his New York studio. When he died in 1896 he was a pauper. Many of his negatives were lost, but some are now preserved in the Library of Congress, Washington.

Meanwhile, in Europe armies were becoming interested in the possibilities of military photography. In England the Royal Engineers set up a small photographic unit in 1856 at the School of Military Engineering, Chatham, and by 1859 the Royal Artillery had done likewise. It was felt that photographers could best be used as a duplicating service, copying maps and plans for distribution among the troops. This photo-copying function continued throughout the century, notably during the American Civil War and in the Franco-Prussian War, when microphotographs were used to reproduce newspapers and messages. Photographs were also useful to record installations and equipment for instructional purposes. Writing of the Royal Artillery photographic unit, *Jackson's Woolwich Journal* of 1 April 1859 says: 'The topographical establishment has had great demands made upon it within the last year in providing the plans and maps connected with the operations of our armies in the Crimea, India, and in China, and in preparing a set of plans of the barracks in the northern district of England.' Photography of troops on active service came very low on the Army's list of priorities, and it is by chance that a good series of photographs taken by the Royal Engineers during the Abyssinian War of 1867–8 still exists. Orders were given that 'a party of one non-commissioned officer and six men of the Royal Engineers, trained photographers, should be attached to the Expedition, with the view of photographing sketches and plans made by Staff and officers'.[10] The party was attached to the 10th Company, Royal Engineers, and £447 6s. 9d. was sanctioned for the purchase of materials. 'The equipment was designed primarily for use as a field printing press', and was packed into eighteen boxes, each approximately 90 lb. in weight, suitable to be carried up-country by pack-mules. A detailed list of equipment included a 'thick, white quilted cover' to protect the camera from the sun, a folding tripod, a portable copying table, a

Dallmeyer Triplet lens suitable for copying plans, and a Chatham tent for use as a dark-room, with an extra white cover to keep it cool. The unit took 15,200 plans and maps for the Engineers. They were lucky in their chief photographer, Sergeant Harrold, who managed to take pictorial views when he could, although the camera was really most suitable for copying documents. Harrold wrote a letter to the *Photographic Journal* of 16 May 1868 telling them of the problems he had as a war photographer. Transport of the heavy photographic equipment was difficult, and 'two of our mules had a regular dance round the camp one day, with a couple of boxes dragging behind them. One of them rolled over on his back three times whilst carrying two of our plate-boxes, and afterwards fell down a place called the Devil's Staircase.' Water was scarce all the time, and dust clogged the camera. The photographic tent was hot and rather unstable in the mountain breezes. He also had personal problems, as he was under orders from officers who did not know anything about photography and often wanted impossible views taken in bad light. In spite of all this, he produced some fine photographs of the campaign. The members of the Photographic Society of London held a lively discussion on Harrold's work. It was suggested that dry plates, recently invented, would be more convenient to use during campaigns, and they debated at length the problems of photography in hot climates, something which most war photographers would have to contend with in the nineteenth century. One of the members, Mr Blanchard, tried to enter into the spirit of the thing by sketching 'the difficulties encountered last summer at Wimbledon when working in an almost tropical heat. Water there was nearly as scarce as in Abyssinia; but whenever possible he made a practice of covering his vehicle with a wet sheet.'[11]

In a review of war photography in Europe between the end of the Crimean War and 1877, when the article was written, the *Photographic Journal* came to the conclusion that photographers had produced little of lasting value. Even at that time, such a short while after the events, many photographs had been lost, and those that had been exhibited had only been seen by a handful of people. Some of the names of the photographers who went to war during this period are known only from the photographic journals. Their motives for going were mixed. 'J.L.' had been in the neighbourhood of the Italian war with Austria by chance in 1859. His photographs have not survived, but his reasons for taking them were admirable: 'I should not like to miss an opportunity of getting a photograph of a field of battle,' so that 'when the excitement of the conflict is past . . . they might not then perhaps talk so flippantly of war.'[12] His first negatives turned out badly, which he attributed to the agitation that the chemicals had undergone on the journey. Later, after taking five negatives, 'a stupid Piedmontese soldier came and lifted up my tent, and thrust his head and shoulders in, knocking down a couple of them which I had stood up to drain, and completing the destruction by laying hold of them with his clumsy paws and rubbing away half the film'. About the same time a French photographer wrote to *La Lumière* saying: 'I shall bring back in my portfolio photographs of all kinds, which would be useful to a painter of battle scenes.' One useful development during this period was the start of aerial photography, first used by Nadar floating 'in a balloon over the field of battle, for the purpose of depicting the manœuvres of the enemy'.[13] Nadar's first experiments were in 1855, and balloon photography for reconnaissance purposes was used extensively from the American Civil War on, until airships and aeroplanes took over in the twentieth century.

Even in 1877 few photographs survived from Bismarck's wars of 1864 and 1866. The *Photographic Journal* mentioned the names of Heinrich Graf, Adolf Halwas and F. Brandt, who took photographs in the Schleswig-Holstein area in 1864, and a Berlin photographer Steihm was awarded a gold medal for his pictures of the 1866 battlefields. Apart from the usual problems, the photographers in Bohemia were hampered by a lack of water, since 'there was not even water for drinking, not to say for making photographs'. Sometimes the final kiss of death was given to photographs of this period by tinting them. The *Photographic News*, reporting on the photographs of the Seven Weeks War of 1866, says: 'Consequently we have no better pictorial mementoes of this glorious campaign than awful pictures coloured with indigo and vermilion.'[14]

Photographs surviving from the Franco-Prussian War and the Commune are particularly disappointing. The *Photographic News* of 1 June 1877 says: 'Of the Franco-German battlefields we hardly remember seeing a single instance. A series of pictures were taken of Strasbourg, during and after its investment, and also of Paris by the German staff of photographers, but those did not include any of the famous battlefields of the war.' The Prussian General Staff raised a 'field photographic detachment' which was commanded by the photographer W. G. Schweier, the unit leaving for Strasbourg on 19 September 1870. They took a closed cart as a dark-room and a transport wagon for apparatus. They completed 116 12″ survey plates, sixteen 8″ × 10″ landscape plates and fifteen stereoscopic pictures, but their work was unappreciated by the Army, and the unit was disbanded six months later. Another photographer at Strasbourg on the instructions of the Prussian General Staff was Johann Baptist Obernetter of Munich, who took 121 pictures of military life on the Paris and Strasbourg fronts. August Kampf was on the Metz front, and published an album of pictures, a copy of which was presented to Emperor Wilhelm I. The *Photographic News* mentions a Mr Meicke, who was with the Prussian Engineer Corps. Because most photographers had to finance themselves and gamble on the chance of selling their pictures, photographic coverage of war during the nineteenth century was haphazard. Towards the end of the century things improved as more war artists and amateurs carried cameras, but it was not until the First World War that there were official Government-paid war photographers.

Numerous photographs were taken in France during the Commune of 1871, but many of these were poor-quality stereoscopic pictures and the names of the photographers were for the most part unrecorded. Several elegiac albums of photographs exist showing damage to the buildings of Paris. One of these was by a landscape photographer, Charles Soulier, and entitled *Paris Incendies*. A. Liebert compiled another volume, *Les Ruines de Paris*. The ruins had a morbid fascination for the Victorians, and parties of tourists came out to see them. Pictures with more interesting subject-matter were described in the *Photographic News* of 1 June 1877: 'Photographs of the barricades thrown up by the Communists in Paris we have also seen, these pictures having a melancholy interest, since the portraits of officers and soldiers included in the photographs served afterwards for their conviction.' These pictures, which were used in evidence against the Communards, could also be tampered with by unscrupulous photographers. A Paris correspondent to the *Photographic News* is quoted as saying that many of the photographs were fanciful and in 'today's papers I see a letter from a lawyer, complaining that his photograph is being sold as that of a prominent member of the Commune, and that he by no means appreciates the joke'.[15] Also circulated were large numbers of faked photographs, supposedly showing Paris burning or the execution of the Communards. These photographs, identical in style with the paintings of the day, were either scenes posed by actors or made up photographically by montage or double exposure. This tendency seemed to go with stereoscopic photography and a certain late-nineteenth-century pixilated humour which enjoyed trick effects with double-exposure ghosts, a style of photography much practised by the London Stereoscopic Co. It was also in the tradition of the genre photographers like Peach Robinson, who carefully posed their photographs and used all kinds of tricks to make them as much like a painting as possible.

The over-sophisticated stereoscopic photographs of the Paris Commune were far removed from the straightforward reporting of the American Civil War. They also had little in common with the numerous pictures taken by British soldiers on campaign during the period. For the British the second half of the nineteenth century is the story of what Kipling has called the 'savage wars of peace'. Continuous warfare became an accepted way of life, usually against an exotic enemy. India was the centre of most of the activity, and Indian army troops were used even if the action was outside the continent. A very competent set of photographs was taken by John Burke during the 2nd Afghan War (1878–80). Burke was a professional photographer in the Punjab who was employed by the Indian Government as a civilian to take pictures of the campaign. A number of professional photographers were available in India at this time who earned their living taking portraits of the troops, occasionally accompanying divisions on punitive expeditions. Burke negotiated his terms, which included a fee, local honorary rank, free carriage and rations for himself and his servants. In return he would supply the apparatus and chemicals. The Government would automatically have six copies of any photographs taken, and Burke would keep the negatives. The Government could call on his services whenever they wanted to. Burke accompanied the 1st Division, Peshawar Valley Field Force, to Afghanistan in 1879 and spent the winter in Kabul with the Army, surrounded by hostile tribesmen. His problems must have been similar to those of Sergeant Harrold twelve years earlier, as his equipment had to be transported through mountainous country, but he also had extremes of cold as well as heat to deal with. His photographs, particularly of the wild country of Afghanistan and the Sherpur Cantonment during the winter of 1879, are remarkably clear and expressive.

Technical advances in photography by the end of the century meant that far more amateurs were able to have cameras with them on campaign. Some lively photographs exist of the Sudanese War of 1898, taken by an officer of the Grenadier Guards. The Spanish–American War and the Boer War are also well covered by amateur photographers. In 1888 Kodak produced the first folding pocket camera incorporating roll film and designed for 'Holiday-makers, Tourists, Cyclists, Ladies, etc.' It was 'mastered in a few minutes' and lived up to the Eastman slogan, 'You press the button; we do the rest'. The machine had fixed focus, fixed stop, one speed, and a dark-room was no longer necessary. Having taken 100 exposures, the camera and film were sent back to the factory, where the film was developed, the camera reloaded and returned with the prints to the photographer. Even generals found time to practise the art. H.C. Shelley, a professional photographer, recalls that General Sir Henry Colvile was interested in photography and had a small quarter-plate camera with him at the Modder River campaign. General Knox was also enthusiastic, and Shelley says: 'The General and I often used the same dark-room at Bloemfontein.' For professional photographers still using a plate camera, dry plates had at last taken over from the laborious wet-plate method. Plates no longer had to be developed on the spot, where they might be damaged by polluted water or heat, and could be sent home for processing under more favourable conditions. This brought its own hazards. During the Boer War one photographer's plates were rudely exposed to the light by the military censor and labelled in violet ink: 'Opened under martial law.' Another lost 300 plates when the steamer *Mexican* sank seventy miles from Cape Town in April 1900.

By the 1890s most of the illustrated journals were printing photographs which were often heavily touched up or painted over, the result looking like a stiffly posed drawing. The exuberance which it was not yet possible to capture photographically was provided by the war artists, who gave lively and misleading representations of fighting, but were still considered superior to photographers. One exception to this was the British magazine *Black and White*, which concentrated on high-quality reproductions of photographs. Some journals had their own photographers or used freelances, but a few versatile men like Rene Bull combined the role of war correspondent, artist and photographer. Bull was a flamboyant figure who first worked for *Black and White* in 1896, sending photographs, drawings and despatches from the Turco–Greek War. Describing these in 1900, *Black and White* said: 'In this campaign his camera played a large part and he was successful on many occasions in portraying scenes of actual fighting, such as had never before been recorded by any artist.'[16] In fact, most of the photographs published at the time seem to be views of Turkey and its people rather than fighting. He described his candid-camera technique, saying: 'I turn my back on the object I wish to photograph, and by opening my left arm a little, I give space to the lens. By the finder on the camera I can tell what I am taking. No one seems to suspect my design.'[17] In January 1898 he accompanied a British force to the Tirah Valley, and sent back 'a batch of photos which I think you will find interesting. An especially interesting one represents Surgeon Major Beeman taking an X-Ray photo of a wounded man's chest to locate a bullet.'[18] He left for the Sudan in February and photographed the aftermath of the Battle of Atbara. 'Of course it was quite impossible to stroll about to find where was the weakest firing, so I just remained where I found myself, watched the progress of the battle, and took my chance.'[19] The pictures credited to Bull of the Battle of Omdurman were probably taken by Lieutenant Loch of the Grenadier Guards. Next he went to South Africa and sent back many photographs, some of which were taken by Horace Nicholls or David Barnett, but not always acknowledged to them. It is difficult to assess Bull's skill as a war photographer, because he often, through accident or design, used other people's work as his own. He was certainly an intrepid newsman and a talented artist, with a knack for self-advertisement.

Many American war correspondents also took photographs during the Spanish–American War of 1898 – in particular, Richard Harding Davis and Burr McIntosh. Others were taken by soldiers in action or by professional photographers, including James Burton and William Dinwiddie of *Harper's Weekly*, James Hare of *Collier's Weekly*, Charles Sheldon, George Lynch and John C. Hemment. Hemment was the aristocrat among them, working for William Randolph Hearst and using one of Hearst's boats as a floating darkroom. Heat caused the usual difficulties and Hemment recalled: 'Making photographs in a tropical climate is trying indeed. . . . In the early hours of the morning the light is beautiful, all one could wish for, but when it comes to dark-room work obstacles in plenty confront you. A good supply of ice is absolutely necessary, provided you wish to have some film remaining on your plates after development.'[20] The damp, humid climate often ruined the plates, and negatives had to be dried with alcohol to prevent the gelatin from sagging. Some of the photographers were beginning to wish that colour photography was possible to capture the tropical landscape of Cuba. It was still not possible to take action shots, as James Burton found out when photographing the Battle of San Juan: 'Almost before I realized what had happened I found myself, for the first time in my life, under fire, right up in front, on the firing line of the 7th Regiment. . . . I found it impossible to make actual "battle scenes", for many reasons – the distance at which the fighting is conducted, the area which is covered, but chiefly the long grass and thickly wooded country.'[21] Some photographers were using the new small box cameras, but John Hemment had a large camera with glass plates. He himself realized that 'Future photographing of war scenes will be done with cameras quite different from those I used in the campaign.'[22]

'The demand for slides connected with the war in South Africa is growing apace,' wrote G.R. Baker in the *British Journal of Photography* on 12 December 1899. 'My advice to those who have pictures applicable to lectures on the war is, publish them, for the martial spirit of the country is aroused and everywhere patriotism is rampant.' The usual select coterie of correspondents, artists and photographers hurried to the scene of action. Rene Bull, representing *Black and White*, was with Buller at the Tugela. Reinhold Thiele, representing the *Graphic*, using a 10″ × 8″ camera with the recently invented Dallmeyer telephoto lens, was with Lord Methuen's Kimberley force. When the *Sphere* started publication in 1900 S.B. Bolas was sent out as photographer, and Hartford Hartland represented *Navy and Army Illustrated* in Natal. In fact, practically all war correspondents, 'whether artists by profession or only writers, carry with them on their perilous mission some form of hand camera', the *Amateur Photographer* reported on 13 January 1900. George Lynch, special correspondent for *The Illustrated London News*, began to send back photographs, all of which needed a great deal of touching-up, in November 1899, and his pictures replaced the far better ones the paper had been using from Horace Nicholls of Johannesburg, a professional photographer. On the South African side David Barnett was one of the most active photographers. He and his brother had lived in Johannesburg for some years and had photographed the Matabele campaign in 1896. The Barnett studios took some of the best photographs of the Boer War. As *Black and White* said: 'Some of the pictures he has sent us have been absolutely unique – notably one, where he showed us the men of a whole regiment climbing a hill in skirmishing order.'[23] Horace Nicholls took some haunting photographs of the Ladysmith campaign. After the war Nicholls settled in England, served in the First World War and later worked for the Imperial War Museum until 1932. Stereoscopic photographs were also still popular, and the American market for these was supplied by Underwood and Underwood, one of whose photographers was H. F. Mackern. A set of their slides of the war, entitled 'For Empire, Queen and Flag', was advertised in the *British Journal of Photography* on 6 June 1900, 'appropriately packed in a box covered with khaki'. The Royal Engineers sent a photographic unit out in December 1899. Second Corporal Ford was appointed tele-photographer and, according to the *British Journal of Photography*, could take a clear photograph up to a range of two miles.[24] The apparatus was made by the London Stereoscopic Co. and was fixed to Ford's bicycle, and the whole thing was painted khaki. The *Daily Mail* of 22 February 1900 mentions that the unit also had two other cameras, including a snapshot machine, and a printing wagon with dark-room and picture gallery. Work by local photographers and amateurs, particularly from the besieged towns, also appeared in print. Cinematograph cameras arrived for the first time at the scene of war. W. K. L. Dickson, with his assistants Cox and Seward of the London Biograph Company, left England on 14 October 1899 in the ship which also carried General Buller and Winston Churchill. Dickson took with him hand cameras as well as his Biograph equipment. The only action scenes that have survived were probably faked back in London on Hampstead Heath. The *British Journal of Photography* rather maliciously draws attention to a sequence supposedly showing the Battle of Colenso: 'We happen to know [these] were taken on Muswell Hill'.

The all-purpose correspondent, artist and photographer of the 1890s was the forerunner of the photo-journalist of the twentieth century. The market for photographs rapidly increased when newspapers started to use them. The *Daily Mirror*, founded in 1904, was the first picture newspaper in the world, and 1919 saw the publication of New York's *The Illustrated Daily News*. The first photographic agencies appeared soon after the Boer War. Equipment was improving all the time. In the mid-twenties a new camera, the Ermanox, with an extremely rapid lens, made fast-action shots in good or bad light possible. The thirties brought in the great age of the picture magazines – *Life* (USA, 1936), *Picture Post* (Britain, 1938) and *Match* (Paris, 1938). Speed of reproduction became essential when rapid transmission of photographs was possible. The old leisurely days of the nineteenth century, when pictures of events sometimes appeared two months later, were over. For this reason there had very seldom been much trouble over censorship then. The propaganda value of war photographs also became more appreciated. Photographs can be as biased as drawings and a more powerful weapon, because they appear to represent the truth. 1900 is a good moment in the history of photography to stop, as after this the story of mass communications gathers momentum. Soon photography was to have an equal place with words in news reports. Now in the 1970s film and television are beginning to take over from still photography. In less than a hundred years the world has moved from the daguerreotype to colour television.

NOTES

[1] *Practical Mechanics' Journal*, 1854
[2] Bentley
[3] *Journal of the Photographic Society*, 21 January 1856
[4] Gernsheim
[5] *Humphrey's Journal*, Vol. 13, p. 133; quoted in Taft
[6] Taft
[7] *Image*, 7 June 1958
[8] Miller
[9] Quoted in Taft
[10] Holland and Hozier
[11] *The Photographic Journal*, 15 December 1868
[12] *Photographic News*, 24 June 1859
[13] *Photographic News*, 17 June 1859
[14] *Photographic News*, 26 October 1866
[15] *Photographic News*, 16 June 1871
[16] *Black and White*, 3 February 1900
[17] *Black and White*, 14 November 1896
[18] *Black and White*, 1 January 1898
[19] *Black and White*, 7 May 1898
[20] Hemment
[21] *Harper's Weekly*, 6 August 1898
[22] Quoted in Freidel
[23] *Black and White*, 3 February 1900
[24] *British Journal of Photography*, 8 December 1899

The full titles of book sources are given in the bibliography.

Bibliography

Anon *Photographic Illustrations of Mandalay and Upper Burma Expeditionary Force* (1888)

Baynes, Ken *Scoop, Scandal and Strife* (1971)

Bensusan, A.D. *Silver Images*

Bentley, Nicolas (ed.) *Russell's Despatches from the Crimea* (1966)

Brown, Sir George *Memoranda and Observations on the Crimea*

Chesney, Kellow *Crimean War Reader* (1960)

Davis, Richard Harding *The Cuban and Porto Rican Campaign* (1899)

Dickson, W.K.L. *The Biograph in Battle*

Edwards, Michael *Battles of the Indian Mutiny*

Edwards, Stewart *The Paris Commune 1871* (1971)

Farwell, Byron *Queen Victoria's Little Wars* (1973)

Forbes-Mitchell, William *The Relief of Lucknow* (1962)

Freidel, Frank *The Splendid Little War* (1958)

Gardner, Alexander *Photographic Sketch Book of the Civil War* (1866)

Gardener, Brian *Mafeking, The Lion's Cage*

Gernsheim, Helmut and Alison *Roger Fenton, Photographer of the Crimea* (1954)

Griffiths, Charles John *A Narrative of the Siege of Delhi* (1910)

Hemment, John C. *Cannon and Camera* (1898)

Hewitt, James *Eye-Witnesses to the Indian Mutiny* (1972)

Holland, Major Trevenen and Hozier, Captain Henry *Record of the Expedition to Abyssinia* (1879)

Horan, James D. *Matthew Brady* (1955)

Horne, Alistair *The Fall of Paris* (1965), *The Terrible Year* (1971)

Hurd, Douglas *The Arrow War* (1967)

Kruger, Rayne *Good-bye Dolly Gray* (1959)

Markham, Charles *The Abyssinian Expedition*

Marshall-Cornwall, James *Grant* (1970)

Miller, F.T. *Photographic History of the Civil War* (1912)

Myatt, Frederick *The March to Magdala* (1970)

National Army Museum *The Army in India* (1968)

Ransford, Oliver *The Battle of Spion Kop* (1969)

Reitz, Deneys *Commando*

Russell, William Howard *My Indian Mutiny Diary* (1959)
Roberts, Brian *The Churchills in Africa*
Selby, John *The Boer War*
Stenger, Erich *The March of Photography*
Taft, Robert *Photography and the American Scene* (1938)
Tisdall, E. E. P. *Mrs Duberly's Campaign* (1963)
Villiers Hatton, Colonel *Diary of the Part Taken by the 1st Battalion Grenadier Guards in the Advance on Khartoum* (1899)
Windham, Sir Charles *Crimean Diary* (1897)
Ziegler, Philip *Omdurman* (1973)

JOURNALS
Amateur Photographer
Black and White
British Journal of Photography
Graphic
Harpers Weekly
Illustrated London News
Image
Jackson's Woolwich Journal
News of the Camp
Photographic News
Photographic Journal

The Photographs

General Sir Charles James Napier (1782- 1853)

2nd Sikh War   1848–9
c. 1848

Photograph by John MacCosh
Copyright : National Army Museum

Portraits of soldiers were the first military photographs taken, and in India especially British photographers began to settle from the middle of the century to take pictures of the British Army in camp, on manœuvres and in action. John MacCosh was a surgeon with the Bengal establishment of the East India Company and took photographs as a hobby. The portrait of General Napier was taken by the calotype process and he would probably have leant against a head-rest of some sort for the exposure of one minute which was necessary. Calotypes, when first produced, were a rich sepia colour, but the image gradually became shadowy. The General's portrait has faded, but it shows an unsoldierly-looking man, with strong features, whose Army career had started in 1794, when he had been commissioned

in the 33rd Foot at the age of twelve. He had led an adventurous life. Lord Dalhousie, who met him about the time the photograph was taken, said: 'What a life he has led, what climates he has braved, how rubbed and chopped to pieces with balls and bayonets and sabre wounds he is!' He had taken part in the Peninsular War and had led a charge at Corunna. He went to India in 1841, writing to a friend before he left, saying: 'I am too old for glory now. . . . If a man cannot catch glory when his knees are supple he had better not try when they grow stiff.' In spite of this, he was responsible for the conquest of Sind, and at the time of the 2nd Sikh War was Commander-in-Chief in India. Napier was sent to replace General Gough. Queen Victoria commented on this in a letter to King Leopold: 'The news from India is very distressing, and make one very anxious, but Sir Charles Napier is instantly to be sent out to supersede Lord Gough, and he is so well versed in Indian tactics that we may look with safety to the future after his arrival.' There were no correspondents at the 2nd Sikh War, let alone photographers, so little was known about it in detail in England at the time.

Indian Artillery Parked Before the Great Pagoda, Prome

2nd Burma War   1852–3
1852–3

Photograph by John MacCosh
Copyright : National Army Museum

By 1852 John MacCosh's photographic skill had increased. He was able to produce calotypes measuring 20·5″ × 21″, as opposed to 10 × 8 cms, the size he was restricted to in the 2nd Sikh War, and so was now able to take views as well as portraits. In January 1852 he was posted to the 5th Bengal Artillery, and sailed with Major-General Godwin's force to attack Rangoon. The attack was a retaliatory measure, as the Burmese had fired on a British frigate which had been sent to the area to protect British merchants from harassment. MacCosh was present at the attack and was able to take photographs of buildings in the city. Prome was taken shortly after Rangoon and the photograph shows the captured Burmese guns. Lord Dalhousie's statement is typical of the motivation for British action in Asia and Africa during the period. He wrote that the Government could not 'appear in an attitude of inferiority or hope to maintain peace and submission among the numberless princes and peoples embraced within the vast circuit of empire, if for one day it gave countenance to a doubt of the absolute superiority of its arms, and of its continued resolution to maintain it'. The war ended with the British annexation of Pegu (Lower Burma), but sporadic fighting continued until 1885 and the 3rd Burma War.

Balaclava Harbour
Crimean War   1854–6
1855

Photograph by James Robertson
Copyright : Victoria & Albert Museum

The long peace in Europe after Waterloo was
broken by the Crimean War. The nominal
cause of conflict was a dispute over rights of
access to the Holy Places, but the underlying
reason was British and French fears of growing
Russian influence in the Balkans. The British,
with France, Turkey and Sardinia as allies,
landed in the Crimea in September 1854. Their
chief objective was to take Sebastopol, a
Russian naval port on the Black Sea. After
fighting the battles of Balaclava, the Alma and
Inkerman, the expeditionary force settled down
to the siege of Sebastopol, with Balaclava as
their supply port. William Russell of *The Times*
described Balaclava when the British first
landed: 'The bay is like a highland tarn, some
half mile in length from the sea, and varies
from 250 to 120 yards in breadth. The shores
are so steep and precipitous that they shut out
as it were the expanse of the harbour, and make
it appear much smaller than it really is.' On the
south-east of the village 'are the extensive ruins
of a Genoese fort, built some 200 feet above the
level of the sea'. The expeditionary force spent a
wretched winter there, with shortages of food
and winter clothing, and an outbreak of cholera
with no adequate medical facilities.

James Robertson, who took this photograph,
arrived at the end of July from Constantinople,
where he was employed as engraver to the
Turkish Mint. The town had been tidied up,
roads built and a hospital (in the foreground of
the photograph), established beside the harbour.
Balaclava had not, however, 'recovered the
picturesque and luxuriant aspect that rendered
it so pleasant as when we landed in October',
wrote an *Illustrated London News* correspondent
on 14 July. 'The almond trees and vines no
longer clustered in the hollows – the meadows
were not green – and though the castle still
adorns the heights, a row of wooden
whitewashed huts makes the mind revert from
reminiscences of the past to the sad realities of
the present. The huts are hospitals for the
wounded, and kind Dr Matthews superintends
the maimed and helpless soldiers who are
brought there from the trenches.'

Roger Fenton's Photographic Van

The Crimean War 1854–6
1855

Photograph by Roger Fenton
Copyright: The Science Museum, London

Roger Fenton's famous photographic van, which served as a portable dark-room and a caravan for Fenton and his assistants, started life as a wine-merchant's van. Fenton converted it before leaving England. 'When it entered into the service of Art, a fresh top was made for it, so as to convert it into a dark room, panes of yellow glass, with shutters, were fixed in the sides, a bed was constructed for it, which folded up into a very small space under the bench at the upper end; round the top were cisterns for distilled and for ordinary water, and a shelf for books. On the sides were places for fixing the gutta-percha baths, glass-dippers, knives, forks and spoons. The kettle and cups hung from the roof. On the floor, under the trough for receiving waste water, was a frame with holes, in which were fitted the heavier bottles. This frame had at night to be lifted up and placed on the working bench with the cameras, to make room for the bed, the furniture of which was, during the day, contained in the box under the driving-seat.' The photograph, with Marcus Sparling in the driving-seat, was taken on the day that Fenton and his assistants made an expedition to photograph 'The Valley of the Shadow of Death'. Fenton said that 'The picture was due to the precaution of the driver on that day, who suggested that as there was a possibility of a stop being put in the said valley to the further travels of both the vehicle and its driver, it would be a proper consideration for both to take a likeness of them before starting'.

The van was a frequent target for enemy artillery, as it was large and painted in a light colour so as not to absorb the heat. The Russians may have thought that it was an ammunition wagon. On leaving the Crimea for England in June, Fenton was able to sell the van for £35.

The Valley of Death

Crimean War   1854–6
1855

Photograph by Roger Fenton
Copyright : Science Museum, London

This was not the scene of the Charge of the
Light Brigade, but 'a well-known spot to all
going down to the trenches, and constantly
referred to in private letters home. It is called
"the Valley of Death" and a most appropriate
name you would say it was.' (*Illustrated London
News*, 30 June 1855.) The valley was in a
dangerous position approaching the heights of
Sebastopol, and under constant bombardment.
William Russell says it received its name after
an incident which took place on 16 October
1854, when a young artillery officer named
Maxwell 'took some ammunition to the
batteries through a tremendous fire along a road
so exposed to the enemy's fire that it has been
called "The Valley of Death"'. It appears to be
a coincidence that Tennyson chose to describe
the scene of the Charge of the Light Brigade by
the same name. The Charge actually occurred
on the plain above Balaclava, not in a valley.

Fenton visited the valley twice. On the first
occasion he said: 'The sight passed all
imagination: round shot and shell lay like a
stream at the bottom of the hollow all the way
down, you could not walk without treading
upon them.' He took his photographs on his
second visit on 24 April. 'I got Sir John
[Campbell] to lend me a couple of mules and
took my carriage down a ravine known by the
name of the Valley of the Shadow of Death. . . .
We were there an hour and a half and got two
good pictures.' The tranquillity of the scene
was quickly shattered: 'It was plain that the
line of fire was upon the very spot I had chosen,
so very reluctantly I put up with another view
of the valley 100 yards short of the best point. I
brought the van down and fixed the camera, and
while levelling it another ball came in a more
slanting direction, touching the rear of the
battery as the others, but, instead of coming up
the road, bounded on to the hill on our left
about 50 yards from us and came down right to
us, stopping at our feet. I picked it up and put
it into the van.'

Captain Brown and his Servant

Crimean War 1854–6
1855

Photograph by Roger Fenton
Copyright: National Army Museum

The Times correspondent, William Russell, was outspoken in his condemnation of the mismanagement of Army supplies at the Crimea during the winter of 1854–5: 'At the commencement of 1855 I could not conceal my impression that our army was likely to suffer severely unless instant and most energetic measures were taken to place it in a position to resist the inclemency of the weather.' Winter clothing for the troops did not arrive. 'I had an opportunity of seeing several lighters full of warm greatcoats etc. for the men, lying a whole day in the harbour of Balaclava beneath a determined fall of rain and snow.' On 16 January the thermometer dropped to 14 degrees in the morning and to 10 degrees on the heights over Balaclava. 'Hundreds of men had to go into trenches at night with no covering but their greatcoats, and no protection for their feet but their regimental shoes.' Many suffered from frostbite. There was little the ordinary soldier could do. The officers dressed in a strange mixture of garments. 'It was inexpressibly odd to see Captain Smith, of the —— Foot, with a pair of red Russian leather boots up to his middle, a cap probably made out of the tops of his holsters, and a white skin coat tastefully embroidered all down the back with flowers of many-coloured silk.' By the time Fenton came to the Crimea the weather had got warmer. Ironically, the winter clothing for the troops arrived about the same time. The soldiers began to look like an army again 'instead of resembling an armed mob, with sheepskin coats and bread-bag and sand-bag leggings and butchers' fur caps'. Fenton wanted to get a photograph of the winter clothing which had been mentioned so frequently by correspondents, so after taking some views 'the foreground of which was formed by the camp of the 4th Light, the officers got their winter dresses out and I made up some interesting groups of them'. Captain Brown of the 4th (Queen's Own) Regiment of

Light Dragoons and his servant wear sheepskin coats described by Fenton as 'the Balaclava livery'. The only regimental garments visible are the blue yellow-striped overalls of his servant.

Lt. Colonel Hallewell, 28th Regiment, his Day's Work Over

Crimean War 1854–6
1855

Photograph by Roger Fenton
Copyright : National Army Museum

Fenton was fortunate in having influential friends at the Crimea. He was on easy terms with the British commanders and had many acquaintances among the officers, who helped to make his stay more comfortable. William Russell found things much more difficult, and Lord Raglan at first denied him the means of drawing rations. Lt.-Colonel Hallewell was an old friend of Fenton's, and is mentioned frequently in his letters to Thomas Agnew. In April 1855 he wrote: 'I went off to Hallewell's tent as I wished to spend the night with him, and roused his servant, who on hearing my name said, "Oh! Sir, Master has been expecting you a long time, he said that if you came I was to make you comfortable." Recommending him to obey his master's orders to the letter, while he went off to tell Hallewell who was dining close by with General Brown I managed very well with a bottle of champagne and ditto of whisky and a box of cigars.' Later: 'We had a very pleasant evening talking of absent friends, and Hallewell became enthusiastic about his recollections of my studio, and our "tête à tête" lasted till 1 a.m.'

On 3 May Fenton wrote of another pleasant occasion with Hallewell: 'In the afternoon I rode with Hallewell to Inkerman, got halfway down the slope, took the bridles off our horses, let them graze, and we lay basking in the sun and looking through the glass at a piquet of Cossacks along the Tchernaya.' On their return Sir George Brown sent for Hallewell to tell him that he had been chosen to go on the Kertch expedition as Deputy Adjutant-General, news which 'made him come home dancing and kicking and emptying a tumbler of champagne'. Fenton accompanied the expedition to the Kertch Peninsula, but took no photographs.

Henry Duberly, Esq., Paymaster, 8th Hussars, and Mrs Duberly

Crimean War 1854–6
1855

Photograph by Roger Fenton
Copyright: National Army Museum

At the time of the Crimean War there was no Pay Corps. Higher finance of the regiment was conducted by regimental agents, who were civilian bankers appointed by the colonels, and the day-to-day affairs were in the hands of regimental paymasters, who had 'honorary' promotion up to the rank of colonel, and twice as much pay per rank as a duty officer. It was traditionally a 'poor officer's' job, and in the case of Henry Duberly might have been considered to be a stepping-stone to the cavalry. In November 1847 Henry Duberly was appointed paymaster to the 8th Royal Hussars with the rank of lieutenant. In 1849 he married, and when the regiment was posted to the Crimea Fanny Duberly was given permission to travel with her husband at

Government expense, together with two other officers' wives. She was a dashing figure and stayed in the Crimea throughout the war and kept a detailed journal. A letter to her sister Selina tells us what she wore about the battlefield: 'You ask me what I wear? Brown holland or cotton gowns – things that will wash. A drab jean habit embroidered [the body] with dark blue – and a white felt hat with a quantity of muslin bound round it. Mrs Cresswell [one of the other wives] swelters in a black habit – it would kill me. I have been obliged to discard all extra petticoats, and have only a gown tail and some linen drawers – and of course no bonnet.' Another letter to her sister referred to the photograph taken by Roger Fenton of Fanny mounted on her horse, Bob, with Henry standing at the horse's head: 'There have been an incredible number of copies [of the photograph] struck off and sold, so I hear. At least, every man I meet seems to have one – and Fenton would not charge us anything for it, I being the only woman.' Fanny Duberly published her journal, but it was considered by Victorian society to be rather unfeminine. She later accompanied her husband during the Indian Mutiny.

Cookhouse of the 8th Hussars

Crimean War 1854–6
1855

Photograph by Roger Fenton
Copyright : National Army Museum

An article in the *Illustrated London News* (13 January 1855) drew attention to the inefficiency of British Army catering methods compared with those of the French. In the case of the French 'one man cooks for twelve, the office falling by rotation; giving all the increased advantages attendant upon division of labour and aggregation of material and resources. The English soldiers cook each for himself as they best can; and the consequence is discomfort and waste.' During the winter there had been almost famine conditions among the ordinary soldiers and the food available could not be cooked due to lack of fuel. With the spring provisions began to get through, and by April M. Soyer was pioneering a hospital kitchen service, and 'portable kitchens' for troops on campaign. It was not until

September 1855 that he gave a demonstration of his equipment, saying that 'the stoves are now in daily use by the Guards and Coldstream Co. where men from other regiments are sent to learn the simple process of camp cookery'.

When Fenton took this photograph cooking methods were much more haphazard. Soup-cauldrons were often made of powder cases, and the soldiers lived on a diet of salt meat, biscuit and rum. The woman in the background was probably one of the soldiers' wives who had come to the Crimea as part of an unofficial corps of wives, acting as washerwomen, needlewomen and camp-workers in return for accommodation. Mrs Duberly, as an officer's wife, was naturally not in this category. The officers were able to have a more elaborate diet, cooked by their servants. A correspondent of the *Illustrated London News* (7 April 1855) enthused over a monumental meal he had while visiting the front: 'We had mutton broth and a sheep's head, salmon and lobster from preserved tins, roast mutton, fowls, ham, capital bread, cheese, loads of sauces, sherry, port and porter; and all of us in capital spirits.'

The wheels of Fenton's photographic van, parked on the left of the group, are just visible.

Camp of the 4th Dragoon Guards: The French and English have a Convivial Party

Crimean War 1854–6
1855

Photograph by Roger Fenton
Copyright: National Army Museum

'Hospitality is certainly one of the most distinguishing features of camp life; everyone offered a welcome, and all had something in the eating and drinking way to offer' wrote a correspondent from Balaclava to the *Illustrated London News* on 7 April 1855. Even during the terrible winter of 1854–5 the French had been much better organized than the British and lived in comparative comfort. Fenton's theatrically posed picture symbolizing Anglo–French solidarity was based on fact, as several eye-witnesses mention the convivial parties which occurred among the troops encamped before Sebastopol during the spring and summer. William Russell said: 'Next day the sun came out, the aspect of the camps changed, and our French neighbours filled the air with their many-oathed dialogues and snatches of song. A cold Frenchman is rather a morose and miserable being, but his spirits always rise with sunshine.' In April a 'Travelling Gentleman' recalled: 'close to us we heard all sorts of jovial singing of old familiar songs; and no set of men could to all appearance have been happier than those besieging Sebastopol, though it was blowing hard and snowing, and at any moment their songs might have been stopped by war in its stern reality.'

Camps of the Light, 2nd and 4th Divisions from Cathcart's Hill on the heights before Sebastopol
Crimean War 1854–6
1855

Photograph by James Robertson
Copyright: National Army Museum

The British encampment on Cathcart's Hill was connected with Balaclava by a road running from the water's edge, up through the village of Kadikoi and along the edge of the plain to the plateau overlooking the naval port of Sebastopol on the other side of the peninsula. Lieut-General Sir George Cathcart, Commander of the 4th Division, wrote to his wife: 'This siege is a long and tedious business. The Russians are making a most gallant defence and we have given them time to prepare for us.' Cathcart was killed at the Battle of Inkerman and the position was called Cathcart's Hill because of the General's habit of using it as a look-out post. He was buried there, a tall stone cross marking his grave in the Officers' Cemetery.

The hill was used by soldiers and civilians alike to watch the progress of the Siege of Sebastopol. In June 1855 William Russell wrote: 'From Cathcart Hill the spectator could see the Flagstaff Batteries' works – the suburb of ruined houses, or rather the sites of cottages and residences, all that was left of long streets destroyed by the fire of our Allies. This mass of ruins was enclosed between the Flagstaff and the crenellated sea wall, and beyond this might be seen the civil town behind, presenting a stately appearance as it rose on the hillside, tier over tier, displaying churches, stately mansions, and public buildings.' On 7 September General Markham told Fanny Duberly: 'Mrs Duberly, we shall have a fight tomorrow. Be up on Cathcart's Hill by twelve.' With other spectators, she watched the assaults on the Malakoff and Redan forts, in danger sometimes from Russian shells directed towards the hill. William Russell was there and offered Mrs Duberly some sherry to keep her spirits up. After Sebastopol was taken 'Even Cathcart's Hill was deserted, except by the "look-out" officer for the day, or by a few wandering strangers and visitors' (William Russell).

Interior of the Redan, left Flank

Crimean War 1854–6
September 1855

Photograph by James Robertson
Copyright: National Army Museum

Mrs Duberly visited the Redan on 13 September, about the same time as Robertson took his photograph. Looking down over the parapet Henry told her that she was standing above the trench where 700 British were buried. Fanny marvelled over the fort: 'What wonderful engineering! What ingenuity in the thick rope-work which is woven before the guns, leaving only a little hole, through which the man laying the gun can take his aim. The Redan is a succession of little batteries, each containing two or three guns, with traverses behind each division; and hidden away under gabions (big round wicker baskets stuffed with earth), sand-bags and earth are little huts in which the men used to live.... Coats, caps, bayonets lay about, with black bread and broken guns. The centre, the open space between the Redan and the second line of defence, was completely ploughed by our thirteen-inch shells, fragments of which, together with round shot, quite paved the ground. We collected a few relicts, such as I could stow away in my habit and saddle-pockets, and then rode down into the town.'

In the early days of the siege, Colonel Windham, who manned an advanced British post, wrote that he was 'within three or four hundred yards of the large Russian battery called the "Redan", and they fire grape and cannister at you at uncertain intervals throughout the night, in the hope of catching someone walking outside the shelter' (December 1854). It was not until September 1855 that Colonel Windham's brigade led the British attack on the fort, at the same time as the French attacked the Malakoff. The Redan was in fact never captured, but the Russians were forced to retreat after the French attack was successful. Souvenir-hunters were soon busy among the ruins of the Redan. A naval officer writing to the *Illustrated London News* noted the 'remains of the desperate struggle – torn red coats, muzzles of muskets, odd

epaulets, ramrods, tailor's gear . . . to say nothing of the most awful of all – the dead. . . . I was very much shocked to see an English lady riding about unconcerned.' This was probably the indefatigable Mrs Duberly looking for souvenirs.

The Interior of Barrack Battery

Crimean War 1854–6 September 1855

Photograph by James Robertson
Copyright : National Army Museum

Battery Barrack was beside the Hospital at Sebastopol and behind the Redan. William Russell, writing about the British assault on the Redan in September 1855, said: 'As the Light Division rushed out into the open, they were swept by the guns of the Barrack Battery and by several pieces on the proper right of the Redan, loaded heavily with grape, which caused considerable loss amongst them ere they reached the salient or apex of the work at which they were to assault.'

The photograph shows the rope mantlets of the Russian guns, which were used to protect their gunners from the destructive fire of sharpshooters. The ground is littered with spent ammunition. Gabions support the parapet on the right. 'These are large hollow cylinders of basket-work, which, being placed on end, and filled with earth, serve to strengthen the faces of batteries. They are generally placed in two rows, one above the other, and should reach to a height sufficient to protect the men in the batteries' (*Illustrated London News*, 16 June 1855).

While Robertson was photographing these scenes, Roger Fenton was already back in England, having stopped off on the way to show his collection of 350 photographs to the French Emperor. The first exhibition of his work was held at the Gallery of the Water-Colour Society in Pall Mall in September, which, coinciding with the taking of Sebastopol, must have proved to be very good for business.

Part of the Barracks held by General Wheeler at Cawnpore after Bombardment

The Indian Mutiny 1857–9
1858

Photograph by Felice Beato
Copyright : National Army Museum

When the Indian Mutiny broke out in May 1857, the fighting was concentrated in north and central India. The key episodes were the siege and relief of the British Residency at Lucknow, the massacre at Cawnpore and the siege and recapture of Delhi. At Cawnpore the Commander, Major-General Sir Hugh Wheeler, tried to defend the garrison for three weeks after native regiments mutinied early in

June. On 26 June he surrendered on the promise of safe conduct from the rebel leader, Nana Sahl, who then brutally massacred men, women and children. This treachery hardened the attitude of the British, who thenceforward responded with equal ferocity.

Felice Beato was primarily a landscape photographer who had worked at the Crimea with James Robertson and normally specialized in Mediterranean views. He came to India at the time of Colin Campbell's relief of Lucknow. His photographs were taken after the battles had been won, and their beautiful composition and precise architectural detail distance the viewer from the horrors of war. In this photograph he has taken the remains of the building held by General Wheeler, with some members of Colin Campbell's force posing among the ruins. An eye-witness, Colonel F.C. Maude, VC, CB, RA, whose album of Beato's photographs is at the Royal Military Academy, Woolwich, said that Wheeler was killed near the broken pillar in the left foreground. Hearn, the Royal Artillery doctor, is the figure on the right. William Forbes-Mitchell, who arrived there on 27 October 1857, some months before Beato, gave this account of the scene then: 'The first place my party reached was General Wheeler's so-called entrenchment, the ramparts of which at the highest place did not exceed four feet, and were so thin that at the top they could never have been bullet-proof. The entrenchment and the barracks inside of it were complete ruins, and the only wonder about it was how the small force could have held out so long. In the rooms of the building were still lying strewn about the remains of articles of women's and children's clothing, broken toys, torn pictures, books, pieces of music, etc. Among the books, I picked up a New Testament in Gaelic, but without any name on it. All the blank leaves had been torn out, and at the time I formed the opinion that they had been used for gun-waddings. . . .'

Interior of the Secundra Bagh

The Indian Mutiny   1857–9
1858

Photograph by Felice Beato
Copyright : Victoria & Albert Museum

The Secundra Bagh was on the outskirts of Lucknow and on the route of Sir Colin Campbell's advance to the relief of the Residency. It was the scene of heavy fighting in November 1857. In his despatch Campbell describes the building as 'a high-walled enclosure of strong masonry, of 120 yards square, and carefully loop-holed all round'. After a fierce battle lasting over an hour and a half, the building was finally taken by a detachment which included the Highlanders, and the 4th Punjab infantry. Campbell reported: 'There never was a bolder feat of arms, and the loss inflicted on the enemy, after the entrance of the Secundra Bagh was effected, was immense – more than two thousand of the enemy were afterwards carried out.' William Forbes-Mitchell recalls: 'the whole seven companies, like one man, leaped over the wall with such a yell of pent-up rage as I have never heard before or since.'

After the action was over the British dead were removed and buried in a deep trench. 'But the rebel dead had to be left to rot where they lay, a prey to the vulture by day and the jackal by night, for from the smallness of the relieving force no other course was possible'.

Subsequently, Lucknow had to be evacuated, and it was not finally recaptured until March 1858. It was soon after this that Beato's photograph was taken. In the courtyard of the Secundra Bagh the corpses of the rebels killed by the 93rd Highlanders and the 4th Punjab Regiment in November still remain. Colonel Maude commented: 'A few of their bones and skulls are to be seen in the front of the picture, but when I saw them every one was being regularly buried, so I presume the dogs dug them up.'

Bridge of boats over the Gumti

The Indian Mutiny 1857–9
1858

Photograph by Felice Beato
Copyright : Victoria & Albert Museum

This may have been the bridge constructed by the Engineers on 5 March 1858 to enable Outram's forces to cross the Gumti River, and thus advance towards the final relief of Lucknow. *The Times* correspondent, William Russell, describes the building of the bridge: 'The engineers are at work on the Gumti, throwing a floating bridge across. . . . Already the men have cut down the bank and made a rough roadway to the water's edge, and the first raft of casks is in the stream.' The bridge is also referred to by William Forbes-Mitchell, who said: 'Early on the 7th March General Outram's division crossed the Gumti by the bridge of boats.'

These bridges were a common sight and Russell referred to two others: one at Cawnpore across the Ganges and another near Allahabad. He gave a vivid description of crossing the latter in November 1858: 'The bridge was dimly lighted by a few lamps fixed to posts on the sides of the boats, which just enabled us to see the planks rising up and down with the surging of the violent current of the black waters passing rapidly away. It was with some difficulty that the horses were induced to trust themselves to the boats. The construction of these bridges is carried to a great perfection in India, where the natives have a traditional method of making them which is said to be superior to the more scientific method of our better-taught engineers. The boats are strongly moored by cables anchored with cross hawsers, and are placed so close together that there is little difficulty in forming a tolerable causeway by means of planks, on which are placed heaps of brushwood, reeds, and earth. But the junction of the bridge with the bank itself is very disagreeable to cross, the banks being steep, and sometimes almost precipitous, and the traffic is so constant that there is almost always a slough of two or three feet deep between the bank and the boats.'

Damage caused by the mine in the Chutter Munzil
The Indian Mutiny 1857–9
1858

Photograph by Felice Beato
Copyright : National Army Museum

The Chutter Munzil Palace was built early in the history of Lucknow for the royal queens. During the Mutiny it formed part of the Residency's defences and was fought over on many occasions. This photograph, taken by Beato soon after the relief of Lucknow in March 1858, shows damage caused by a mine exploded by the mutineers during Havelock's advance six months earlier. Both sides took part in mining and counter-mining operations and could often hear each other at work. William Russell mentioned the occupation of the palace during the final British advance on the Residency on 16 May 1858: 'As we approached the shattered walls of the Residency, a few shots were fired from the buildings; but there was no show of opposition as the 23rd and 79th extended and entered the enclosure. By a movement of a portion of the force to the right, the Chutturmunzil, the Mohtec Mahal, and the other palaces on the bank of the Gumti, were occupied.'

Lieutenant Mecham and assistant surgeon Thomas Anderson with Sikh Officers and Men

The Indian Mutiny 1857–9
1858

Photograph by Felice Beato
Copyright : National Army Museum

Clifford Henry Mecham served at Lucknow in defence of the Residency from June to November 1857 with Hodson's Horse, the regiment raised by Lieutenant Hodson during the Mutiny. After the garrison was relieved in November, he took part in the campaign in Oudh during 1858 and at this time his photograph was taken by Beato. Thomas Anderson, the other British officer in the group, qualified as a doctor in Edinburgh in 1853 and became an assistant surgeon in the Army in 1854. He had been present at the siege and capture of Delhi. The officers and members of

the Sikh Horse photographed with them have been posed carefully by the photographer to avoid movement with the long lens exposure that was necessary. Mecham manages to look particularly nonchalant.

The Sikhs, recent enemies of the British, were loyal during the Mutiny, and played an important role in the campaigns to relieve the Residency at Lucknow. An officer who saw them parade before Colin Campbell on 11 November 1857 said: 'Wild and bold was the carriage of the Sikh cavalry, riding untamed-looking steeds, clad in loose fawn-coloured robes, with long boots, blue or red turbans and sashes, and armed with carbine and sabre.' William Russell rode with a Sikh on 10 March 1858, the day after the Sikhs made a successful assault on the Martinière with the Highlanders: 'The old Sikh, stroking his beard, which flowed almost down to his saddle, told us tremendous fibs' about the fighting. 'He was a noble-looking old economist of the truth, and his men were the wildest, finest-looking fellows possible.'

Pehtang Fort and encampment of Probyn's Sikh Cavalry

Chinese Wars 1856–60
August 1860

Photograph by Felice Beato
Copyright : Victoria & Albert Museum

The long drawn-out Chinese wars extending from 1856 to 1860 were caused by the British desire to trade freely with China and to have diplomatic representatives in Peking. There was constant friction between the two countries, due to the illegal importation of opium by British merchants. War first broke out in 1856, when members of the crew of a British-registered trading vessel, the *Arrow*, were seized. In retaliation, the British shelled Canton and destroyed the forts on the approach to Peking. The Chinese hastily sued for peace, but the treaty was never ratified and trouble broke out again in 1859. The first attempts to take the forts of Pehtang and Taku, which were on the direct route to Peking, were unsuccessful. A new attempt was made, in alliance with the French, in 1860, and on 1 August British and French troops landed at Pehtang, a small town on the coast about ten miles from Taku. The landing was difficult, as it involved wading through up to two miles of mud to get ashore. The Chinese retreated and left the Pehtang forts undefended, although mined.

Probyn's Horse was raised during the Indian Mutiny as the 1st Regiment of Sikh Irregular Cavalry. The regiment fought under Major D.M. Probyn during the Mutiny. Indian corps of irregular cavalry were particularly suitable for service in China, as they would 'eat and drink whatever you give them, are hardy and robust, accustomed to a climate much like their own' and were not given to looting.

The photograph is part of a two-negative panoramic view of the interior of the fort and of the town, and the flat, desolate country by the side of the Pehtang River. The photographer, Beato, probably travelled out with one of the Indian regiments, arriving in time for the capture of Peking.

56

Pehtang Fort, with captured Chinese Guns

Chinese Wars   1856–60
1860

Photograph by Felice Beato
Copyright : Victoria & Albert Museum

Another view of Pehtang fort soon after it was
taken by the British, with one of the captured
Chinese field-guns in the foreground. The war
artist and correspondent of the *Illustrated
London News* described the capture of the fort:
'There was no resistance at all; and the forts
soon appeared with the French and English
flags floating in the evening breeze. No
preparation seemed to have been made for a
defence; a few wooden guns were found, and
some infernal machines. . . . The forts are built
of mud and chopped straw, beautifully neat, and
finished off to perfection in a pyramidal style,
two truncated pyramids, and a perpendicular
square fort at the top; the walls are crenellated.
The town, land, and water all of the same
colour.'

Embrasure, Taku Fort

Chinese Wars   1856–60

Photograph by Felice Beato
Copyright : National Army Museum

Once Pehtang had been taken, the next move
was to march from the town to Sinho and the
Peiho River. The forts of Taku guarding
Peking could then be tackled. These four forts,
two either side of the Peiho River, were well
defended, and had caused heavy casualties
during the unsuccessful attack in 1859. On
21 August the allies attacked the northern fort,
backed up by the artillery. On 1 May 1860
Jackson's Woolwich Journal had said: 'Should
Lord Elgin not be able to arrange our
difficulties with them on amicable terms, there
can be no doubt that the Armstrong gun will
prove an efficient peacemaker.' This prophecy
was correct. 'The fire of the artillery was most
effective, the guns of the fort (of which many
were of very large calibre) were speedily
silenced and at about 7 a.m. the magazine blew
up with a terrific explosion.' Four hundred guns
were captured. The elaborate system of
obstacles that the Chinese had built round the
forts made retreat difficult and their bodies
were strewn round the interior of the forts.
Beato's photograph was taken shortly after the
attack, and the British scaling ladders can be
seen on the left of the gun embrasure. An
arrow rocket used by the defenders is on the
parapet.

Rear of the North Taku Fort after its Capture

Chinese Wars 1856–60
1860

Photograph by Felice Beato
Copyright: Victoria & Albert Museum

News of the war in China travelled slowly to the British newspapers. It was not until 31 November that a report on the taking of the Taku forts appeared in the *Illustrated London News*: 'The Taku Forts were captured on the 21st August, after five hours' hard fighting at the northern forts. The others surrendered. The enemy was allowed to march out, leaving munitions, etc. The allies lost 400 men killed and wounded. No British officer was killed. The 67th and 44th Regiments and the Marines, with 1,500 French, were the troops principally engaged. The Allied Plenipotentiaries arrived at Tien-Tsin on the 26th. They would start shortly for Pekin, escorted by Cavalry.'

Jackson's Woolwich Journal (1 December 1860) had an interesting description of the construction of the Taku forts. All were 'redoubts, with a thick rampart heavily armed with guns and wall pieces, and having a high cavalier facing seawards, the guns of which were all turned in towards us; they have two unfordable wet ditches, between which and the parapet sharp bamboo stakes were thickly planted, forming two belts, each about fifteen feet wide, round the fort, an abattis encircling the whole, and further covered by pieces of water, which force an advance to be made only on a narrow front.' After the attack on 21 August 'the ground outside the fort was literally strewn with the enemy's dead and wounded – three of the Chinese were impaled on the stakes'. Six Victoria Crosses were awarded for the storming of the North Taku fort.

With the forts destroyed, the British gunboats advanced up the River Peiho. Peking surrendered in October and Beato was able to take a photograph of Prince Kung, who surrendered the city on behalf of the Emperor.

Yankee Prisoners from Bull Run in Castle Pinckney, Charleston, South Carolina

American Civil War 1861–5
August 1861

Photograph by George Cook
Copyright : Valentine Museum, Richmond, Virginia

The American Civil War brought an abrupt change in the style of photography. The Brady-trained team of photographers was able to get much closer to the fighting and to take vivid pictures with immediate impact, in complete contrast to Beato's formal, impersonal views. There was no great difference in the photographic equipment used. Glass plates, usually 8″ × 10″, were taken into the field with all the difficulties attendant on wet-plate development. George Cook, although now working for the Confederate side, was an ex-employee of Brady's and had once managed his New York studio.

The secession of the southern states from the Union to form the Confederate States of America on 1 February 1861 led to the Civil War. The twenty-three north and west states under Abraham Lincoln wished to restore the Union and to abolish slavery, on which the southern economy was based. The Confederates, who made Richmond their new capital, wanted their independence to be recognized. The North believed that the war could be ended quickly, but after Federal setbacks in 1861, including the 1st Battle of Bull Run, realized that their troubles would not be over so quickly. Castle Pinckney was a fort in Charleston Harbour, and here were brought Federal prisoners taken at Bull Run in July 1861. The prisoners photographed were members of the 79th (Highlanders) Regiment of New York City and the 8th Michigan Regiment. The uniform of the 79th was dark blue, with a small red stripe on the trousers and jacket. On their caps was the number '79' in brass figures. Most of the coatless men in the picture belonged to the 8th Michigan Infantry. Their guards were the Charleston Zouave Cadets, seen on the parapet. This was a company of Confederate boy soldiers, all residents of Charleston, who had joined up directly the state of South Carolina seceded from the Union. Their uniform was grey, with red stripes and trimmings, red fatigue-caps and white cross-belts. Later in the war they saw action at the front. No escapes have been recorded from Castle Pinckney, so these Federal troops may have remained there throughout the war, unless they were later part of a prisoner-of-war exchange with the Confederates.

Inspection of Troops at Cumberland Landing, Pamunkey VA.

American Civil War   1861–5
May 1862

Photograph by Wood and Gibson
Copyright : British Museum's copy of Gardner's
Photographic Sketch Book of the Civil War

The main impetus to photograph the Civil War had come from Matthew Brady. In the early days of the war he had financed photographic expeditions to the front, arranged for all the negatives to be printed and had publicized the prints under his name. Alexander Gardner, Brady's partner from pre-war days, was still in 1861 the most important member of his photographic team, and was at this time official photographer to the Army of the Potomac. Among other members of the Brady team accompanying the Army of the Potomac on their Peninsular Campaign were Wood and Gibson, who took this photograph. Brady was himself also present at some of the engagements.

General George B. McClellan's Army of the Potomac landed at Fortress Monroe early in 1862 with the intention of sweeping up the peninsula between the York and James rivers to besiege Richmond. Having taken Yorktown and Williamsburg, the Army gathered at White House, near Cumberland Landing, to prepare for the final assault. Cumberland Landing, on the Pamunkey River, was the Army's supply base, where steamers and barges gathered to bring equipment and food from Fortress Monroe. The Army camped here from 15 to 19 May. The empty fields beside the river were converted to an 'immense city of tents stretching away as far as the eye could see'. In this photograph 'the prominent object is a mud-bespattered forge, the knapsacks and blankets of the farriers carelessly thrown on the ground beneath'. Mules are feeding on the right, and to the left of them the guard sit beside their knapsacks and stacked muskets. Beyond them a cook sits on a mess-chest, close to the ashes of his fire. The 5th New York Volunteers, Warren's Zouaves, are encamped on the edge of the wood and a regiment of infantry is drawn up in front of the tents for inspection.

Savage Station: Union field hospital after the Battle

American Civil War   1861–5
30 June 1862

Photograph by James Gibson
Copyright : Library of Congress, Washington DC

The Army of the Potomac advanced from Cumberland Landing towards Richmond at the end of May. 'The march was a picturesque one, through a magnificent country arrayed in all the gorgeousness of a Virginia spring, with its meadows of green set between the wooded hills. Dotted here and there could be seen the mansions of planters, with their slave quarters in the rear.' (Henry W. Elson) Fierce fighting took place at Fair Oaks on 31 May and in the Seven Days' Battles during the last week of June, covering the Federal retreat to a new base at Harrison's Landing. At one time McClellan's army had been able to hear the clocks striking in Richmond, but they were unable to take the city and were at last beaten back with heavy losses. The engagement at Savage Station took place on 29 June, when the 2nd and 6th Corps of the Federal Army repelled an attack by the Confederate General Magruder. The next day the Union troops retreated into the White Oak swamps, leaving their medical officers behind to deal with the wounded.

Medical arrangements were rough-and-ready at the beginning of the war and each regiment did the best it could. Medical equipment was often at the rear of the line and inaccessible in case of emergency. There were no antiseptics and soldiers did not carry dressings into action. The injured man covered his wounds as best he could with a dirty handkerchief or piece of cloth torn from a sweaty shirt. The wounded photographed here are waiting dejectedly to be taken prisoner. The picture was taken just before the rearguard withdrew, presumably taking the photographer with them. When the Confederates occupied Savage's Station on the morning of 30 June 2,500 sick and wounded men and their medical attendants became prisoners-of-war.

Dead by the Railway fence on the Hagerstown Pike, Antietam

American Civil War 1861–5
17 September 1862

Photograph by Alexander Gardner
Copyright : Library of Congress, Washington DC

After the Confederate victory at 2nd Bull Run, General Robert E. Lee turned north to invade Maryland. He was met at Antietam in western Maryland by McClellan's Army of the Potomac. This photograph was taken beside the railway fence on the Sharpsburg to Hagerstown turnpike, where General 'Stonewall' Jackson attempted to rally his men in the face of the furious Federal attack which opened one of the bloodiest battles of the Civil War on 17 September 1862 at Antietam. General Hooker's batteries opened fire on the Confederates, who were drawn up in a cornfield adjoining the fence in the photograph. After their bombardment,

Hooker's troops advanced. 'Back and still farther back were Jackson's men driven across the open field, every stalk of corn in which was cut down by the battle as closely as a knife could have done it. On the ground the slain lay in rows precisely as they had stood in ranks.' (Miller) The Confederates rallied and soon the railway fences were festooned with the corpses of both sides and the cornfield was soaked with blood. 'The two lines,' said General Palfrey, 'almost tore each other to pieces.'

When the photographs of Antietam were first published, Brady received the credit for all of them. Among their admirers was Oliver Wendell Holmes, who wrote: 'These terrible mementoes of one of the most sanguinary conflicts of the war, we owe to the enterprise of Mr Brady of New York.' It was only after the war that Gardner got the credit he deserved for his Antietam photographs.

Dunker Church and the Dead, Antietam

American Civil War   1861–5
17 September 1862

Photograph by Alexander Gardner
Copyright: Library of Congress, Washington DC

One of the best photographs taken at the Battle of Antietam was this view of the dead in front of Dunker Church. The church, which was on a ridge near Sharpsburg, was the central landmark of the Confederate lines, and when the rebels were driven from the cornfield beside Hagerstown Pike, they fell back to positions beside the church. 'The slaughter here was fearful. Each of the contending lines charged repeatedly across the field in front of the building, and strewed the ground with their dead.' (Miller) Shot-holes can be seen in the church and the dead lie beside one of the guns. Some boots in the right foreground of the picture have probably been removed from one of the bodies to be taken away as loot. The Confederates had been positioned behind the church when the King's Division under General Hatch attacked them. Battery B, 4th U S Artillery, lost heavily during the course of the engagement. Finally, the Artillery commander, Lieutenant Stewart, sent two guns to the rear and took up a position with the four remaining guns on a knoll near a sunken road. They opened fire on the rebels, 'the discharge from the four twelve pounders sweeping out half a dozen panels of the fence, and driving a storm of slugs and shotted rails into the mass of Confederates. The rear still pressed on, ignorant of the havoc in front, and again and again the artillery poured its iron hail into the column, completely obstructing the road with dead and wounded.' (Miller) Oliver Wendell Holmes, who visited the battlefield at the same time as Gardner to search for his wounded son, wrote: 'Let him who wishes to know what war is look at this series of illustrations. The wrecks of manhood thrown together in careless heaps or ranged in ghastly rows for burial were alive but yesterday.'

Signal Tower on Elk Mountain, overlooking the battlefield of Antietam

American Civil War 1861–5
October 1862

Photograph by Timothy O'Sullivan
Copyright : British Museum's copy of Gardner's
Photographic Sketch Book of the Civil War

Elk Mountain is in the South Mountain Range of the Blue Ridge, and from the summit almost the entire Antietam battlefield could be seen. The Signal Station was operated by Lieutenants Pierce and Jerome, and O'Sullivan has posed the picture to show Pierce receiving a dispatch from General McClellan. A Confederate correspondent, writing in a Richmond paper, said: 'Their signal stations on the Blue Ridge commanded a view of our every movement. We could not make a manœuvre in front or rear that was not instantly revealed to their keen look-outs; and as soon as the intelligence could be communicated to their batteries below, shot and shell were launched against our weakest points, and counteracted the effect of whatever similar movements may have been attempted by us.' The corps of signallers was of particular value at Antietam. Federal signal officers were placed at intervals along the line of battle and reported on the movements of the enemy by means of flags. It was the message received from this station, 'Look well to your left', which enabled General Burnside to guard his position against A.P. Hill's advance from Harper's Ferry.

Timothy O'Sullivan was another distinguished member of the Brady team who later joined Gardner and stayed with him for seven years.

A Harvest of Death, Gettysburg

American Civil War 1861–5
July 1863

Photograph by Timothy O'Sullivan
Copyright : British Museum's copy of Gardner's
Photographic Sketch Book of the Civil War

After the crushing defeat of the Union troops at Chancellorsville, Lee advanced northwards and invaded Pennsylvania. His army almost reached Washington, but was intercepted by a stronger Union force at Gettysburg under General Meade, who had replaced Hooker. In a three-day battle the Confederates attempted to break the Union lines, but Lee's army was forced to fall back to the Potomac, and it was clear that the tide had turned in the Union's favour. O'Sullivan's picture was one of the most famous photographs shot during the war and had a profound effect on contemporary imagination. It was taken after Lee's army retreated and the bodies were soaked with rain, which had been falling for two days. 'Swept down without preparation, the shattered bodies fall in all conceivable positions. The rebels represented in the photograph are without shoes. These were always removed from the feet of the dead on account of the pressing need of the survivors. The pockets turned inside out also show that appropriation did not cease with the coverings of the feet. Around is scattered the litter of the battlefield, accoutrements, ammunition, rags, cups and canteens, crackers, haversacks, etc., and letters that may tell the name of the owner, although the majority will surely be buried unknown by strangers, and in a strange land.' By the time the photograph was taken some of the Union soldiers had already been buried and in the background Federal troops can be seen exploring the battlefield.

The Aftermath of Sedgwick's assault on Marye's Heights

American Civil War 1861–5
3 May 1863

Photograph by A.J. Russell
Copyright : Library of Congress, Washington DC

After Antietam McClellan was relieved of his command and replaced by General Burnside, and the Army of the Potomac advanced on Fredericksburg. Marye's Heights was a strong Confederate position in the hills behind the town, fought over first in December 1862 when the Federal troops were driven back. The position was attacked again in the Chancellorsville campaign in May 1863 by the new commander for the Army of the Potomac, General Joseph Hooker. Sedgwick's 6th Corps was ordered to take Marye's Heights again. At 11 a.m. on 3 May the Federal troops advanced, supported by flanking fire. 'Up to within twenty-five yards of the wall they pressed, when again the flame of musketry fire belched forth, laying low in six minutes 36·5% of the 5th Wisconsin and 6th Maine.' (Miller) There was fierce hand-to-hand fighting and the Confederates were driven from the rifle pits and the guns were captured. The photograph, taken by A. J. Russell on the day after the battle, shows the destruction caused by a shell from the 2nd Massachusetts' siege gun battery, which was positioned across the river at Falmouth. It has overturned Confederate caisson wagons and killed the horses and men. General Herman Haupt, Chief of the Bureau of Military Railways, leans on a tree stump surveying the scene. Beside him is W.W. Wright, Superintendent of the Military Railroad. Lee recaptured the position on 4 May and the Federal forces again withdrew from Fredericksburg. Matthew Brady was present at the Chancellorsville campaign and got most of the credit when the photographs taken there were later exhibited. Russell had worked for Brady at one time and was a captain in the Union army.

Council of War,
Massapomax Church
American Civil War 1864–5
21 May 1861

Photograph by Timothy O'Sullivan
Copyright : Library of Congress, Washington, DC

Early in 1864 Grant was made commander of all
the Union armies, and in a series of engagements gradually wore down the main
Confederate force. His troops were now near
the Confederate capital, but Lee held a strong
position at Cold Harbor, ten miles north of
Richmond. O'Sullivan managed to get a
photographic scoop by climbing upstairs in a
roadside meeting-house and photographing
Grant's Council of War in the courtyard below.
He took a series of three photographs to get the
impression of movement, an idea which was
used later by Gardner in his photographs of the
hanging of the Lincoln conspirators. General
Horace Porter, who was present at the

conference, later identified the participants.
General Grant leans over General Meade's
shoulder and consults his map. In front of them
an officer bends forward to receive orders.
General Porter is bending over to pass papers to
another officer and the rest of the group look at
Grant. Soldiers from the 3rd Division of the 5th
Army Corps, whose wagons are passing, stop to
watch. According to General Porter, the
question was: 'Whether to attempt to crush
Lee's army on the north side of the James, with
the prospect, in case of success, of driving him
into Richmond, capturing the city, perhaps
without a siege, and putting the Confederate
Government to flight; or to move the Union
army south of the James without giving battle
and transfer the field of operations to the
vicinity of Petersburg.' Grant made the costly
decision to fight, with the result that 7,000
Federal troops were killed or wounded. In his
memoirs Grant said: 'I have always regretted
that the last assault at Cold Harbor was ever
made.'

'Mortar Dictator' in Front of Petersburg

American Civil War 1861–5
October 1864

Photograph by David Knox
Copyright : British Museum's copy of Gardner's
Photographic Sketch Book of the Civil War

Next to Richmond, Petersburg was the most important Confederate military centre in Virginia. It was also an important supply centre and the junction for five railways. It was surrounded by Union forces from June 1864, but not finally taken until April 1865. This 13″ mortar with a 200-lb. exploding shell was made by Charles Knapp at the iron works in Pittsburg, and was used in the siege operations in front of Petersburg. It was so large that it was mounted on a railway car and ran on the Petersburg and City Point Railroad to a position known as Battery 5, where a curve in the track made it easy to change the direction of the fire when necessary. It terrorized the Confederates and succeeded in silencing their batteries on Chesterfield Heights. Its activities were directed by Colonel H.L. Abbot of the 1st Connecticut Heavy Artillery, who is photographed standing in the left foreground beside the gun. Next to him is General H.J. Hunt, Chief of Artillery. 'Some shots from this gun went much farther than they were ever intended, carrying their fiery trails over the Confederate entrenchments and exploding within the limits of the town itself, over two and a quarter miles. The roar of the explosion carried consternation to all within hearing.'

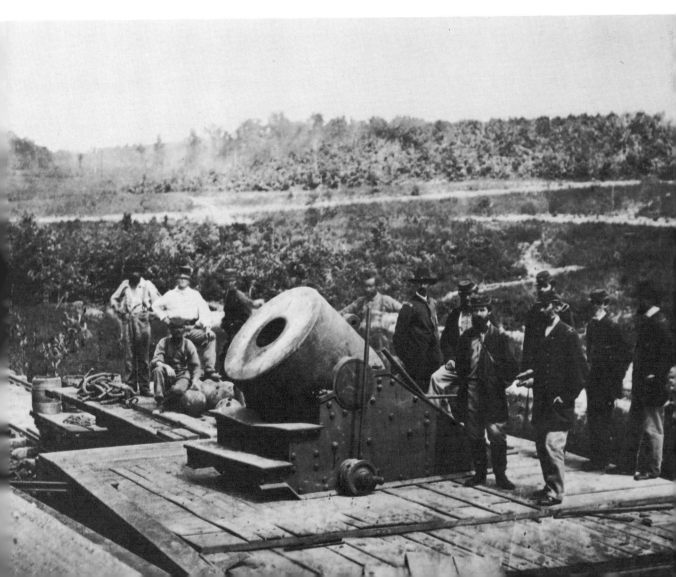

Cooper's Battery ready to open fire

American Civil War   1861–5
June 21 1864

Photograph by a Brady assistant
Copyright : Library of Congress, Washington DC

After the disaster at Cold Harbor, Grant decided that it was best to drive Lee back towards Richmond and capture the Confederate capital. To do this he first marched to Petersburg which lay between Richmond and the rest of the southern states. The siege of Petersburg lasted for ten months and cost the Federals 42,000 casualties and the Confederates 28,000. Fifty years afterwards James Gardner described the circumstances in which this photograph was taken for Miller's *Photographic History of the Civil War*. Battery B, 1st Pennsylvania Light Artillery, known as Cooper's Battery, 'arrived in front of Petersburg on June 17 1864, was put into position on the evening of that day, and engaged the

Confederate batteries on their line near the Avery house.' Gardner, himself a photographer, was a lieutenant in the Battery, and remembered Matthew Brady and his assistant arriving to take photographs on June 21st. 'The Confederate guns frightened Brady's horse which ran off with his wagon and his assistant, upsetting and destroying his chemicals.' Brady can be seen in the centre of this photograph wearing civilian clothes and a straw hat. The Pennsylvania Battery 'suffered greater loss than any other volunteer Union battery' during the war; 'its record of casualties includes twenty-one killed and died of wounds, and fifty-two wounded – convincing testimony of the fact that throughout the war its men stood bravely to their guns.'

Federal Soldiers relaxing by Guns of a Captured Fort, Atlanta
American Civil War 1861–5
1864

Photograph by George Barnard
Copyright : Library of Congress, Washington DC

Atlanta was occupied early in September 1864 as part of General Sherman's campaign to subdue Georgia. Sherman then moved on to the sea, destroying stores, railroads and property on a sixty-mile front. Savannah was captured in December, and Columbia and Charleston soon followed. The photograph shows a Confederate fort at the end of Peach Tree Street, Atlanta, to the north of the city, with Sherman's troops in occupation.

George Barnard was an Army photographer working under Captain Poe, the Chief Engineer of the Military Division of the Mississippi. His usual work was to photograph maps, but he also made an important series of war photographs when he accompanied Sherman on his march to the sea. A picture in Miller's *Photographic History of the Civil War* shows Barnard at work inside the new Federal fortifications constructed by Captain Poe's division at Atlanta from September to October 1864. The photographic wagon which carried his chemical supplies is beside him. He also had a small light-proof tent so that he could sensitize his plates and then develop them after taking the photographs. Barnard took a series of photographs of these new fortifications which were later sent to Washington by Captain Poe.

Federal Wagon trains move through Petersburg

American Civil War 1861–5
April 1865

Photograph by J. Reekie
Copyright: Library of Congress, Washington DC

There is a strangely deserted air about the town of Petersburg in this photograph. Taken early in the morning, it shows the Federal wagon trains moving through the quiet streets while Union guards line the route. Grant's troops had at last taken the city after months of siege and the inhabitants were probably disinclined to watch their conquerors pass through the town, although the photographer, J. Reekie, managed to record the moment from the upstairs window of his house. The wagons contained supplies for Grant's army, which was pursuing the Confederates as they moved westward up the Appomattox Valley. News of the fall of Petersburg came to Jefferson Davis at Richmond on 2 April. Richmond could not now be held and the arsenals and public buildings were burnt before the Confederate Government left the city. On 7 April Grant wrote to Lee: 'The results of the last week must convince you of the hopelessness of further resistance on the part of the Army of Northern Virginia in this struggle.' The two Generals met at Appomattox Court House and Lee surrendered.

Execution of the Lincoln Conspirators in the Arsenal Penitentiary Courtyard, Washington D.C.

American Civil War 1861–5
7 July 1865, 2 p.m.

Photograph by Alexander Gardner
Copyright : International Museum of Photography,
George Eastman House, New York

Less than a week after Appomattox, President Lincoln was murdered on 14 April 1865. Alexander Gardner was in Richmond photographing the ruins of the town when he heard the news and hurried back to Washington to take pictures of Lincoln's corpse. He also took portraits of the conspirators held at the Arsenal Penitentiary. These portraits later appeared as engravings in *Harper's Weekly* for 13 May 1865. On 7 July, from a balcony overlooking the courtyard of the Penitentiary, he took a series of photographs of the prisoners as they were led past their open graves and made to mount the scaffold. In this picture Surratt, Powell, Herold and Atzerodt hang lifeless. *Harper's* also published these photographs as engravings.

Matthew Brady was strangely inactive at this time, although some of his photographs of Lincoln's funeral procession exist. Gardner also took pictures later of the hanging of Wirz, the Confederate commandant of Andersonville prisoner-of-war camp, another series of photographs with great news value.

F

Inside the Lower Battery at Simonosaki after the Fighting

Japan 1864
6 September 1864

Photograph by Felice Beato
Copyright : John Hillelson Agency

Japan suffered in the same way as China from attempts by Western powers to open up trade. Japan's isolationism was resented and in

October 1852 the *Edinburgh Review* wrote: 'The compulsory seclusion of the Japanese is a wrong not only to themselves, but to the civilized world. . . . The only secure title to property, whether it be a hovel or an empire, is, that the exclusive possession of one is for the benefit of all.' In 1858 a treaty was negotiated to enable foreign diplomats and trading representatives to enter the country, but there was a good deal of hostility towards the foreigners; murders were committed and reparations demanded. Finally, a joint British, French, Dutch and American force sailed to bombard the batteries on the

Simonosaki Straits in 1864. The *Illustrated London News* noted in December 1864 that some sketches 'by Mr Wirgman and photographs by Signor Beato of Yokohama' had just arrived which showed the action of 5–6 September 'between the allied British, French, and Dutch squadrons and batteries and land forces of the Prince of Nagato'. A force under Captain Kingston of *Perseus* and Lieutenant de Hort of the Dutch ship *Medusa* captured the Lower Battery unopposed on 5 September. 'Finding that the battery had been abandoned by the Japanese, the assaulting party spiked the guns, and returned without molestation to their ships.' This rare photograph by Beato shows the French from the *Seramis* occupying the other battery on the following day. 'The Japanese guns are pointed at extreme elevation; they are cast in Jeddo, and the carriages are likewise of Japanese manufacture.' In the background some of the English officers look on. Captain Alexander of the *Euryalus* stands next to the man with the flag. On 14 September there was a truce, and a new commercial treaty was finally negotiated in June 1866.

Capture of the Düppel Redoubt

German-Danish War   1864
1864

Photographer unknown
Copyright : Staatsbibliothek, Berlin

Very few pictures have been preserved of the
first of Bismarck's wars fought to achieve the
unification of Germany under Prussian
leadership – the German–Danish War of 1864
and the Seven Weeks War of 1866. Perhaps if
the conflicts had lasted longer photographers
would have made their way to the front. The
majority of pictures taken may well have been
lost soon afterwards, as there was no demand
for prints. The Duchies of Schleswig and
Holstein had been a source of friction between
Prussia and Denmark for some years, and in
1864, after making an alliance with Franz Josef
of Austria, Bismarck occupied the territories.
The Danes fell back to their second line of
defences in the Alsen Sound and the Düppel
fort. 'Here, perhaps, their position will put
them somewhat nearer to an equality of
strength with their foes, by contracting their
line of operations and allowing them to make
use of their naval armaments', commented the
Illustrated London News, definitely on the side
of the under-dog. Düppel was on the Baltic side
of Schleswig at the end of the Sundewitt
Peninsula, and the Prussians besieged it
vigorously from February until May 1864. A
Danish correspondent, writing to the
Illustrated London News on 17 March, said:
'The Prussians fired about 350 shots on
Tuesday, 500 yesterday, and probably a larger
number today. The bastions on the Dybbol
[Düppel] position suffered no material harm –
none, at least, that could not immediately be
repaired. The loss of life was, however, severe
on the part of the Danes. . . . The sentries of
the hostile armies are so close that they might
hand each other tobacco.' On 18 April a
Prussian army of 40,000 men, 'after many days'
profuse cannonade and bombardment of the ten
redoubts on Düppel Hill, at length took them
by an easy assault, the Danes being greatly
overmatched'. . . . 'The forts, which were
already almost demolished, became heaps of
sand and earth, and the gun carriages were shot
to pieces.'

84

Inside The Düppel Redoubt

German-Danish War   1864
1864

Photographer unknown
Copyright: Staatsbibliothek, Berlin

The military strength of the Prussian Army had been created by the Army reforms of Roon, Minister of War, Moltke, Chief of the General Staff, and Bismarck, the political leader who emphasized the need for Prussia to have a strong army if she was to be accepted as a great power. Universal liability for military service was enforced, and the infantry were equipped with the Dreyse needle-gun. The most up-to-date breech-loading Krupp artillery was used. Moltke became Chief of the Prussian General Staff in 1857 and perfected Army administration. The Danes were no match for the Prussians. After retreating from Düppel, the last stages of the war were fought around Fredericia, which was taken on 29 April, and the Danes were forced to sue for peace. By the Treaty of Vienna the Danish King ceded his rights over Schleswig-Holstein to the two victorious German powers, but two years later there was war again, this time between the two Allies. The third of Bismarck's wars of German unification was the Franco–Prussian War of 1870–1.

The Mule lines at Zula

The Abyssinian War   1867–8
1867

Photograph by Sergeant Harrold, RE
Copyright : Institution of Royal Engineers

Part of a panoramic view on three negatives of
the base camp at Zula, this photograph was
taken by the newly formed photographic unit
attached to the 10th Company, Royal
Engineers, under Sergeant Harrold. It had been
necessary for Britain to send a military
expedition to Abyssinia as the British Consul,
88

Captain Charles Duncan Cameron, had now
been held prisoner by the mad King Theodore
for nearly three years, and the party sent
recently to negotiate his release had also been
imprisoned. A landing was made in Annesley
Bay at Zula in October 1867. It was a desolate
area, but there was fresh water, and it was in a
sheltered position for landing supplies and
troops. Inland were the mountains through
which the expedition would have to go to reach
Magdala, where the prisoners were held. Men
and equipment, artillery and ammunition
poured into Zula. A huge transport corps was
organized to take everything on the rough

journey through the mountains to the interior, and mules, horses, bullocks and camels all had to be deposited at Zula. A number of elephants, which greatly impressed the Abyssinians, were also sent from Bombay. Captain Atkinson of the 45th Regiment, who sent some of Harrold's photographs back to the *Illustrated London News*, reported: 'At the landing steps of "the old Pier", a stirring and bustling scene meets the eye: men of various nations are hurrying to and fro, some employed in loading trucks with stores and provisions of all sorts; others in disembarking cattle, mules, camels and elephants.' Muleteers had to be recruited and

the animals fed and watered. On the right of the photograph are stacked pack-saddles for mules, probably of the McMahon type, described by Charles Markham as 'a structure between a hatchway ladder and a hen-coop'.

Harrold used wet-plate photography throughout the trip, although he had brought some dry plates with him in case of emergency. The extreme heat made conditions for photography adverse in the Annesley Bay area, and 'great vigilance was necessary to preserve the collodion of the proper consistence and to avoid the desiccation of the plate when taken from the bath'. (*Photographic Journal*, 15 December 1868)

General Napier with Officers of the Royal Engineers

The Abyssinian War 1867–8
1868

Photograph by Sergeant Harrold, RE
Copyright : Institution of Royal Engineers

Sir Robert Napier was appointed to take charge of the Abyssinian expedition on 14 August 1867, and ordered to 'make a peremptory demand for the delivery of the captives, and to follow it up by such measures as he thinks expedient'. He arrived at Annesley Bay on 2 January 1868 and the march to Magdala began in February. His mission was delicate, and its chief purpose the rescue of the hostages. After a difficult journey through the mountains, Magdala was reached in April, the hostages freed and the fortress stormed. Theodore the King committed suicide. The return march was uncomfortable, as the weather was bad and

Bulago Camp

The Abyssinian War 1867–8
1868

Photograph by Sergeant Harrold, RE
Copyright : Institution of Royal Engineers

Sergeant Harrold and his photographic unit did not stay long in Zula, but marched up-country to Senafe, 'views of the mountain passes being obtained en route; and here he remained with his staff for a short time, taking extensive photographic sketches of the camp and environs'. (*Photographic Journal*, 16 May 1868) In February they joined the march to Magdala. Their work was often to duplicate plans and maps, 'printed upon salted paper and mounted upon linen; and the work is done so rapidly that it frequently happened that their prints were produced and distributed within twenty-four hours of the receipt of the original plans'. Sometimes the unit had to fall out of the line of march to develop and print their films. Difficulties were great. 'Often the maps were blown right off the copying-table; and during exposure it was frequently necessary to keep brushing the dust and sand from the original.' Bulago Camp was 230 miles inland from Zula and 151 from Magdala. At this point the tracks were particularly bad and the mountains steep.

90

sickness was beginning to trouble the forces, who were suffering from a sense of anticlimax. They began to cheer up as at each camp rations were increased. 'Rum appeared again and was heartily welcomed in Wadela; new boots and chocolate in Ashangi; damson jam, currant jelly, and mixed biscuits at Antalo; beer at Adigrat; and at Senafe there was a street of Parsee shops abounding in every kind of luxury.' (Frederick Myatt, *The March to Magdala*) On 30 April General Napier issued his farewell order to his troops, congratulating them on crossing 'ranges of mountains – many steep and precipitous, more than 10,000 feet in altitude, where your supplies could not keep pace with you. In four days you passed the formidable chasms of the Beshilo, and when within reach of your enemy, though with scanty food, and, some of you, even for many hours without either food or water, you defeated the army of Theodore which poured down upon you from its lofty fortress in full confidence of victory.'

Harrold was able to take some views and photographs of native chiefs on the journey, apart from the photo-copying and map work, but was unable to obtain a photograph of King Theodore. 'An order was sent down by General Napier to obtain a picture of the fallen chief, but owing to some delay the instructions were not given to the Engineers until after the internment; the authority for visiting the body reached Sergeant Harrold one hour late.' His photographs on the historic occasion include views of Magdala and King Theodore's house, and pictures of some of the rescued hostages. The photograph of Bulago Camp was probably taken on the return journey, when the photographers had more time, and the returning expedition reached there on 6 May. Even then the photographers were still under orders from officers who were ignorant of photographic matters. 'Sometimes the mules had to be halted and the boxes unpacked during a long march in a drizzling rain in order that a picture might be attempted of some mountain or other, the top of which was enveloped in a dense fog, simply because a staff officer had expressed himself to the effect that the whole would make a grand picture.' (*Photographic Journal*, 15 December 1868) It was remarkable, considering the limitations, that such competent photographs were taken.

The Battle of Sedan, showing Prussian troops in attacking formation

Franco-Prussian War   1870–1
September 1870

Photographer unknown
Copyright : Radio Times Hulton Picture Library

By 1870 the French had been one of the leading powers in Europe for eighty years, but only ten years earlier Prussia had been one of the least of the countries to be reckoned with. Now Prussia was strong enough under Bismarck to declare war on France on 15 July 1870. The Prussians inflicted a crushing blow on the French six weeks later at Sedan, virtually defeating them, although the armistice was not signed until January of the following year. The French army, under the personal command of the Emperor, had been marching to the relief of Metz, where 170,000 French troops were trapped. The Prussian 3rd Army met them at the fortress of Sedan, near the Belgian border, and the French defeat ended any hope of the relief of Metz, which capitulated on 27 October. Describing the Battle of Sedan, the *Illustrated*

London News said: 'The French had repeatedly attempted, in the course of that fatal day, to break through the circle which Von Moltke had directed to be drawn round them. But every attempt was defeated, till the mass of disordered troops – no longer an army but a mob of soldiers – was forced to take shelter under the walls of the fortified city. Then, about 5 o'clock in the afternoon, the white flag of surrender was sent out to the King of Prussia, and the terrible struggle was past.' Among the 82,000 prisoners was Napoleon III.

If this photograph is authentic, it is one of the first to show actual fighting. Unfortunately, it is much more likely to have been a fake, and much of the detail has probably been painted in, as the distant figures of the soldiers are much too distinct for the cameras of the time. If nothing else, it shows the kind of battle photograph that the public had always expected to see. The picture is part of a collection bought by the *Radio Times Hulton Picture Library* from Henry Guttman of Paris.

Fort Issy

Franco-Prussian War 1870–1
1 February 1871

Photographer unknown
Copyright: Radio Times Hulton Picture Library

Paris was encircled by the Prussians in
September 1870, and a siege of four months
followed. The city was surrounded by an
encircling wall 33′ high, with ninety-four
bastions, and a moat 10′ wide. There were
fifteen detached forts outside, barring the
approaches to the city, and Issy was on the
south of the Seine, forming part of a group with
Ivry, Bicetre, Montrouge and Vances. These
particular forts were uncomfortably overlooked
by the heights of Châtillon to the south. Once
the bombardment by the Prussians commenced
the guns of Issy were gradually silenced. Early
in January 1871 the *Illustrated London News*
reported: 'The barracks of Fort Issy were burnt
by Prussian fire on Wednesday. . . . The
population are reported to be most resolute
notwithstanding that many shells have fallen
into the town.' A week after: 'The Germans
have established rifle-pits within 800 yards of
Issy, and are likely enough to sap up to it in
another week.' By 11 January: 'Prussian fire
today was directed almost exclusively against
the southern ports, and more especially Fort
Issy, which was the object of an incessant
cannonade.'

The photograph was taken soon after the
surrender with victorious German troops inside
the ruined fort. The trials of Issy were not yet
over, as it became the scene of fighting again
during the Commune, when the insurgents took
it for a period. On 5 May one of the National
Guards in the fort wrote: 'All our trenches,
smashed in by artillery, have been evacuated.
The Versailles parallel is within 60 metres of
the counter-escarpment.' Two days later: 'We
are now receiving up to ten shells a minute.
The ramparts are completely uncovered. . . .
With the exception of one or two, all the guns
have been knocked out.' There was little left of
the fort when Government troops reoccupied it
in May, and an observer described it as little
better than a heap of rubble, with the parapet
a shapeless mound.

A Cannon on the Butte Montmartre

Paris Commune   1871
1871

Photographer unknown
Copyright : Radio Times Hulton Picture Library

Owing to the heavy bombardment and starvation conditions, Paris surrendered on 28 January 1871. Elections were held for the National Assembly, and it became clear to the extreme left wing in Paris, who had not accepted defeat, that the propertied classes and the provinces were determined to negotiate an armistice with Germany. Just before the Germans marched into the city, crowds led by the National Guards removed the cannons, which had been collected together by the Government on the Place Wagram, and dragged them away to other sites, including the Heights of Montmartre. The National Guards felt that the guns were their property, as many bore National Guard numbers and had been bought by public subscription during the siege. On 18 March Thiers gave orders for the Regular Army to recover the guns. The attempt was repulsed and on 28 March the Paris Commune was proclaimed.

This photograph shows the National Guards beside one of the cannons during the Commune period. The *Illustrated London News*, valiantly trying to put its readers in the picture, describes the position of La Butte Montmartre in Paris as similar to that of Primrose Hill in London! It went on to say that, since resisting the Government's attempt to recover the guns, the National Guards had 'converted La Butte Montmartre into a formidable redoubt, and parked the guns, with the ammunition-waggons behind, along the steep, winding road towards the summit of the hill'. In fact, the eighty-five cannons were allowed to deteriorate and were not adequately manned and the Government were able to take the position quite easily on 27 May, when the Commune was overcome.

96

Execution Scene

Paris Commune   1871
1871

Photograph by E. Appert
Copyright : Radio Times Hulton Picture Library

This is a cleverly faked photograph showing the
execution of Generals Thomas (left) and
Lecomte (right) on 18 March 1871. Thomas was
Commander of the National Guard, and after
rebel Guardsmen captured the Montmartre
guns they also took prisoner their hated
commander. Thomas was much disliked for his
part in crushing the 1848 Revolution, and more
recently was blamed for the high casualties
suffered by the Guard at Buzenval. General
Lecomte had been detailed to recapture the
guns for the Government and was dragged from
his horse to be executed after his own troops
defected. The two men were shot in the garden
of 6 Rue des Rosiers, Montmartre. There was
no proper execution squad and the mob rushed
from the place 'into the streets in the grip of
some kind of frenzy. Among them were
chasseurs, soldiers of the line, National Guards,
women and children. All were shrieking like
wild beasts', wrote Clemenceau, an eye-witness.
The photographic scene was set up soon after
the execution and the heads of the two generals
printed in on the bodies of other men later.
These faked photographs were very popular in
France at the time. They were made by the
stereoscopic process and sold in large
quantities.

Communards Beside the statue from The Fallen Vendôme Column

Paris Commune 1871
May 1871

Photographer unknown
Copyright : Radio Times Hulton Picture Library

The Vendôme Column was considered by the Commune to be a symbol of repression and the glorification of war, and so singled out for destruction. This grandiose act with great popular appeal was open to many interpretations, Freudian and otherwise, but was carried out with comical thoroughness by the Communards. The Column had been erected by Napoleon in Roman style to commemorate the victories of 1805. 16 May was the day appointed for its destruction and a huge crowd turned out to see the fun. The Communards attacked the Column as if it was a tree and tried to saw through the stone and bronze. Ropes were attached to the top and were pulled by sailors and members of the National Guard. 'Several layers of faggots, straw and stable manure were placed along the roadway for some distance up the Rue de la Paix to receive the column when it fell.' Bands played the 'Marseillaise' and everyone watched from the windows. 'It fell (after some difficulty) exactly on the litter prepared for it, with a dull, heavy, lumbering sound.' (*Illustrated London News*, 27 May 1871) There was a tremendous cry of '*Vive la Commune*' and a man planted a red flag on the pedestal and made a speech.

This picture shows a group of Communards posing for their photograph by the statue of Napoleon in a toga, which had been on the top of the monument. 'It was curious to see this massive figure – with its firm, calm, immobile face – staring up to the skies amidst the eager, turbulent, and half-maddened crowd.' It was unfortunate for some of the Communards that they had posed for their picture, as many were later traced by the Government from photographs.

A Barricade in the Place Vendôme

Paris Commune 1871
March 1871

Photographer unknown
Copyright : Radio Times Hulton Picture Library

It was in keeping with Paris revolutionary traditions to erect a barricade for the defence of a 'quartier', where local people would fight to protect their own district. During '*la semaine sanglante*' between 22 and 28 May, the last stand of the Commune was made on the barricades. Unfortunately for the Communards, the placing and strength of the barricades was not effective in keeping back the Government troops. The barricade photographed here in the Place Vendôme was a flimsy structure built out of square cobblestones dug up from the street. The National Guardsmen pose proudly beside their gun. The National Guard had started as a citizen militia, but in 1870, when more troops were needed to guard Paris, the Government did away with restrictions limiting entry to members of the *bourgeoisie* and opened its ranks to everyone. Numbers quickly rose to 3,000,000, but the men were not properly trained and lacked proper equipment, and soon became a potent revolutionary threat.

When the Government troops first entered Paris on 21 May, the Communards believed that many would fraternize with them and were not prepared for the butchery which followed. *Figaro* said that the Communards were savage beasts, and encouraged the Versailles troops to hunt them down 'without pity, without anger, simply with the steadfastness of an honest man doing his duty'.

British Cavalry and Artillery awaiting the arrival of Amir Yakub Khan to sign the Peace Treaty at Gundamuk

2nd Afghan War 1878–80
May 1879

Photograph by John Burke
Copyright : National Army Museum

One of the methods used by the British at this time when they wished to control the affairs of an Asian or African country which they had no taste for conquering was to offer a subsidy and demand that a British resident or mission should reside at the Court. This usually worked in India, but the Afghans had other ideas, and instead approached Russia. Fear of Russian influence in the area caused the British to invade Afghanistan in 1878. The advance was made on three fronts. General Sir Donald Stewart made an unopposed march from Quetta through northern Baluchistan to Khandahar, Lieut-General Sir Samuel Browne moved into the Khyber Pass and Major-General Roberts attacked through the Kurram Valley, fighting the Battle of Peiwar Kotal. Sher Ali gave in, and on his death in February 1878 was succeeded by his son, Yakub Khan, who finally agreed to negotiate peace terms in May 1879. It was first arranged that the British peace mission, headed by Major Sir Louis Cavagnari, would meet the Amir in Kabul, but anti-British feeling was so strong in the capital that it was feared that the safety of the British mission could not be guaranteed. The Amir agreed to come instead to the British camp at Gundamuk, where he was received with royal honours.

John Burke, a professional photographer in the Punjab, took this series of photographs of the campaign. He had got permission to accompany the 1st Division, Peshawur Valley Field Force, and arrived in time to record the signing of the Peace Treaty, soon to be broken by the murder of Cavagnari.

Peace talks between Amir Yakub Khan, General Daob Shah, Habeebula Moustafi and Major Cavagnari and Mr. Jenkyns

2nd Afghan War   1878–80
May 1879

Photograph by John Burke
Copyright : National Army Museum

Yakub Khan arrived in Gundamuk on 8 May 1879 wearing a striking uniform designed in the fashion of 'some dress worn by a German, or most probably a Russian sovereign'. Resplendent in coat and trousers of white cloth heavily embroidered with gold, holding his gold helmet with a plume of feathers, he quite outshone the other members of the peace commission. The treaty was signed on 26 May, and gave the British control of Afghanistan's foreign policy and the right to have British agents in the country. The Kurram was ceded to Britain, together with control of the Khyber Pass and the tribes living in the area. Major Cavagnari became the first Resident and took up his quarters in Bala Hissar with a small staff. In spite of the treaty, the Afghans were not at all convinced that they had lost the war.

Major-General Roberts recalls that he had forebodings and did not feel equal to proposing a toast to the mission at the farewell dinner: 'I was so thoroughly depressed, and my mind was filled with such gloomy forebodings as to the fate of these fine fellows, that I could not utter a word.' Scarcely four months after taking up his appointment, Cavagnari was murdered, and the war started up again.

The war artist of the *Graphic* made drawings of Burke photographing the peace talks. 'Mr J. Burke, the photographer artist attached to our Indian Army to illustrate the advance of the troops and the grand scenery of Afghanistan, was permitted by the Ameer of Cabul to take a series of pictures of himself and his suite at the camp at Gandamak. One of my sketches illustrates the process of "posing" the Ameer, who indulged in a quiet smoke during the preparation of the photographic plates. . . . The Ameer showed great anxiety to see the results, and Major Cavagnari explained to him the process of photography.' In the first drawing Burke can be seen using a large camera on a tripod with a white frilly parasol fixed over it to give protection from the sun. In the second sketch he is washing the glass plate surrounded by an admiring group, consisting of the Amir, Cavagnari and other distinguished members of the peace mission.

Guns captured from Ali Musjid on Shergai Heights

2nd Afghan War   1878–80
1879

Photograph by John Burke
Copyright : National Army Museum

The fort of Ali Musjid was captured by a British force under Lieut-General Sir Samuel Browne on 22 November 1878. The fort guarded the Khyber Pass, which was at that point only 150 yards wide, and its capture had been a considerable British victory. The captured guns were brought down to Peshawar on 5 December, where they were later photographed by Burke. The *Graphic* describes in detail the transport of the guns to Peshawar: 'Each of the large guns was drawn by six of the large oxen that are employed in the heavy siege train battery belonging to Peshawar,

and the smaller guns and howitzers, with their carriages, were borne on the backs of six large elephants of Major Wilson's elephant battery. Most of these guns, which were of brass, had a beautiful finish, and were all made at the Ameer's foundry in Cabul, excepting one which had been given to the Ameer by the English and had an English inscription on it; there were some 7-pdr. 3-grooved rifle guns, and some 9-pdr. The Afghans made very good practice with these pieces, for they killed and wounded nearly fifty of our soldiers at the taking of their fort at the Khyber Pass.'

Major-General F.E. Appleyard, who commanded the 3rd Brigade, 1st Division, Peshawar Valley Field Force, is in the left foreground with some members of his staff. He had been present at the attack and capture of Ali Musjid. His previous service had been with the 80th Regiment in the Burmese War of 1852, and he had also taken part in the Crimean Campaign, 1854–5.

Captured guns of Kabul parked in Sherpur

2nd Afghan War   1878–80
1879–80

Photograph by John Burke
Copyright : National Army Museum

When the British occupied Kabul in October 1879 they also took possession of the Amir's artillery and ammunition park. Other guns which were found abandoned on neighbouring hills were also brought in. 'Eighty-five guns and mortars were found in the Bala Hissar, together with a large quantity of arms and ammunition

for Snider rifles, the ammunition apparently manufactured in the country' reported *The Illustrated London News*. The Royal Artillery had lost a number of their guns during the 1st Afghan War, so in some cases they were recapturing their own. Others had been given to the previous Amir by the British Government. 'Among the guns captured during the campaign were a complete battery of siege guns presented to Sher Ali some years ago by the British Government. This battery consisted of four smooth-bore 18-pdr. and two 8-inch howitzers.' Among the ammunition found was about '200 round shot and 160 common shell for the howitzers'.

Sherpur Cantonment: The Laager and Abbattis

2nd Afghan War 1878–80
23 December 1879

Photograph by John Burke
Copyright: National Army Museum

News of the murder of the British mission reached Simla on 5 September 1879, providing a photographic scoop for Burke, whose picture of the peace mission appeared as a drawing in the *Graphic* to illustrate the sad event. General Roberts returned at the head of 10,000 men to avenge the deaths. After defeating the Afghan army at Cherasia, he entered Kabul in mid-October, following the abdication of the Amir. Winter had now to be spent in Kabul, and it was decided to use the Sherpur cantonment, as Roberts's force was small and the position could be defended. Sherpur was a huge fortified enclosure. It could easily contain half the city of Kabul within its walls. The British force was invested for ten days by 100,000 Afghans, who were repulsed on 23 December after heavy fighting, and put to flight. Burke's photograph, showing the north-west corner of Sherpur, illustrates with remarkable clarity the conditions there during the winter. Guns encircle the British position, with branches of trees beyond them as added defence. The 5th Punjab Infantry is in position. In the background are the Bemaru Hills.

H.Q. Signalling camp in the Engineers' Park

2nd Afghan War   1878–80
1879–80

Photograph by John Burke
Copyright : National Army Museum

The Royal Engineers in Afghanistan were responsible for the supervision of any field engineering work required. The work was carried out by Madras, Bengal or Bombay sappers and miners, who were Indian personnel commanded by officers and NCOs of the Royal Engineers. They were also responsible for instructing other arms in electric and visual methods of signalling, as there was no independent Signals Corps until 1920. During the 2nd Afghan War the main method of communication between units was by heliograph, and some twenty-four stations were set up. The heliograph, an example of which can be seen in front of the tent on the right, was a circular mirror on hinges which reflected rays of the sun and so transmitted morse signals. In Afghanistan the rugged country made the work extremely difficult and dangerous. Flags were also used for visual signalling and a lantern was employed at night. The man in the centre of the photograph appears to be using a plotting table. Indian troops stand around, and the British soldiers are wearing an assortment of clothes and headgear to combat the cold.

A Group of Field Telegraphers

2nd Afghan War   1878–80
1879–80

Photograph by John Burke
Copyright : National Army Museum

As the Kurram Valley Column advanced into Afghanistan some 170 miles of telegraph wire was laid. For the Kandahar column 140 miles was completed and 108 for the Khyber column. Most of the work was carried out by civilian employees of the Indian Government, but their stores and equipment were most probably carried by the Field Engineers' Parks, which were manned by Royal Engineer sapper and miner personnel. The *Illustrated London News* noted on 29 November 1879: 'The telegraphic communication between Cabul and Peshawar is completed. . . . The *Standard* of Wednesday first published the telegrams of its correspondents at Cabul and Candahar dispatched on Tuesday, which marks a great improvement in the expeditious transmission of news.' In the centre of Burke's photograph a soldier is transmitting morse. Mr Josephs, the Superintendent of Telegraphs, presumably a civilian, is on the left. On the right Indian soldiers hold the wire, and two telegraph poles can be seen dimly in the background, but the wires have vanished into the sky, as it would have been difficult for a camera to pick them out at this period.

G Battery, 3rd Royal Artillery

2nd Afghan War   1878–80
1879–80

Photograph by John Burke
Copyright : National Army Museum

On 17 October 1878, G Battery of 3rd Royal
Artillery, commanded by Major Sidney Parry,
then stationed at Rawalpindi, was placed under
orders for active service. On 30 October the
Battery joined the Kurram Division of the army
of the invasion under General Roberts. Part of
the Battery was left at Kohat and the rest, under
Major Parry, marched on 16 November to Thal
and crossed the Kurram River on 23 November.
On 2 December they took part in the attack on
Peiwar Kotal. After the retreat of the Afghan
Army, a battery was left to form part of the
garrison of Peiwar Kotal. The Battery then
went to Ali Khal, where it remained until the
Peace of Gundamuk, when it returned to the
Valley. When hostilities commenced again in
the autumn the Battery left Kurram on 25
September and took part in the attack on
Kabul. They were in the Sherpur cantonment
throughout the winter and did not return to
India until August 1880.

Field Artillery and R.H.A. Officers and N.C.O.s

2nd Afghan War 1878–80 1879–80

Photograph by John Burke
Copyright : National Army Museum

A description of the Field Artillery guns written probably about the time the photograph was taken said: 'The field artillery attached to Sir F. Roberts's force consists of six muzzle-loading rifled 9-pdr. guns of F Battery A Brigade of Royal Horse Artillery, six similar but slightly heavier guns belonging to G Battery 3rd Brigade Royal Artillery, four 7-pdr. mountain guns, Morgan's Battery, and the same number of Swinley's – in all, twenty guns.' The Royal Horse Artillery had been with Brigadier General Burrows at the Battle of Maiwand in 1880, when they had run out of ammunition and had been surrounded, but had managed to save the guns. They had fired the salute when the British flag had been raised at the capture of Kabul in 1879 and were in Sherpur during the winter of 1879 to 1880.

Bala Hissar gate

2nd Afghan War 1878–80
1879–80

Photograph by John Burke
Copyright : National Army Museum

The light in Afghanistan must have been
particularly clear for Burke to have been able to
take this superb panoramic view of the fortress
of Bala Hissar at Kabul. Bala Hissar was almost
a complete town, as its walls enclosed nearly a
quarter of the city. The Amir's palace was here
and also the British Residency, which was
stormed and burnt in September 1879. Kabul
was occupied by Roberts in October, and his
remarks are evidence of the romantic
associations that the area had for the Indian

Army: 'At last I was at Kabul, the place I had
heard so much of from my boyhood, and had so
often wished to see.' Some punitive executions
took place and Roberts intended to destroy
Bala Hissar as a warning to the Afghans, but
fighting broke out again and he was reluctantly
compelled to retire to Sherpur for the winter.

Burke probably took this photograph in the
autumn shortly before the British withdrew to
Sherpur, leaving the fortress to the Afghans.
All Burke's photographs taken at the Afghan
campaign are outstanding for the period. The
Zulu War, which was taking place at the same
time, had no such talented photographer, and
the pictures taken there are uninteresting. India
was generally better served photographically
than elsewhere because there were many
experienced photographers earning their living
there by taking pictures of the British Army.

'News of the camp' Offices, Pretoria

1st Boer War 1880–1
1880–1

Photograph by H.F. Gros, Pretoria
Copyright : Royal Commonwealth Society

In 1877 the British annexed the Transvaal and
in December 1880, after failing to get
independence by political means, the Boers
besieged British garrisons, which were not
relieved until after the Armistice. In Pretoria
the Administrator, his staff and British troops
retired to the Fort, taking with them British
residents and shopkeepers. The 'Fort' was a
brick building, with a ditch round it, situated in
an open plain on the verge of the racecourse,
about a mile outside the town. Here, to keep up
the spirits of the garrison, one of the officers,
Charles Du Val, started a newspaper called
News of the Camp with a colleague, Charles
Deecker. The Editor's quarters were an Army
bell tent and a transport wagon with the space
in between roofed in with a tattered sail
stretched on telegraph poles. They edited the
paper by day and did guard duty by night, 'up
to the knees in mud, at night, save when
sleeping in leather breeches, long boots, and
jack spurs, with a bandolier as a necklace, a bag
of cartridges for a bolster, and a Snider carbine
for a sleeping partner', as the *Daily News*
(London) eloquently described it. Their aims
were to retail 'gossip and general chit chat' of
the camp to 'the beleagured inhabitants of
Pretoria'. They ran into trouble with the first
issue on 25 December 1880: 'This day's issue is
only one-quarter of the size the journal usually
will be, as the pouring rain has penetrated
through our canvas roof and sadly interfered
with the harmony of our arrangements.' In
spite of difficulties, they continued to publish
throughout the siege.

The photograph of the *News of the Camp*
offices comes from an album belonging to
the Royal Commonwealth Society. In March
1881 Charles Duval told his readers that he was
intending to issue bound copies of the journal
once the siege was over: 'The Proprietors have
made special arrangements with Mr H.F. Gros,
by which subscribers for their bound volumes

can be supplied with photographs of the
principal objects of interest in the camp and its
surroundings at the rate of 30s. per doz for the
large, and 18s. per doz for the small pictures.
. . . The photographs will be specially printed to

avoid the warping so general, and instructions
for pasting in will also be supplied.' The copy
held by the Royal Commonwealth Society also
contains some letters from Du Val.

H

Tents of Nos. 2 and 3 Companies, Convent Redoubt

1st Boer War   1880–1
1880–1

Photograph by H. F. Gros, Pretoria
Copyright : National Army Museum

Convent Redoubt was one of the four small forts which protected the main garrison at Pretoria. 'Notes from the Convent Redoubt' appeared frequently in *News of the Camp*. On 31 December 1880: 'Some facetious friends in one of the companies have dubbed their tents the "Albemarle Hotel, Piccadilly", and another "Boer Scare Cottage". . . .' 8 January 1881: 'The men have now got well shaken down to camp life; the officers have got their Mess established at last, and everything all round is more shipshape and orderly.' 'We feel it rather a

hardship that we never have a chance of hearing the evening performance of the R.S.F. Band, and if the rule about gate closing could be relaxed for this purpose it would be esteemed a great boon by all here.' A polo match is reported on 27 January which resulted 'in a severe cropper for Captain Churchill, whose pony – making a beautiful X with his forelegs – came down and rolled his rider in quite a happy manner.'

There were sporadic attempts of the Army to break out throughout the siege, but, lacking cavalry, they were able to do little against the skilled horsemanship of the Boers. There was considerable depression following the Boer victories at Laing's Nek and Majuba Hill, and by March the *News of the Camp* reported that 'the hearts of the defenders have sunk to zero'. An armistice soon followed and the Transvaal recovered its independence, which was lost in 1877.

The Medical Staff

3rd Burma War   1885–6
1886–7

Photograph by Colonel R.B. Graham,
7th Bengal Cavalry
Copyright : Royal Commonwealth Society

In three minor conflicts between 1824 and 1886 Britain had slowly gained control in Burma, operating from India. This photograph comes from a unique album belonging to the Royal Commonwealth Society. The book was privately printed, with original photographs stuck in as illustrations, and was the work of Colonel Graham of the 7th Bengal Cavalry. In the Preface he gives his reasons for the collection: 'When I first commenced taking Photographs in Burmah, it was more for my own satisfaction, but later on, when I found so many of my friends were anxious to secure copies, which I had not the time to print, it struck me that they would probably be glad to obtain a series, as a memento of Burmah, if I could get them done at a moderate price. The pictures are necessarily small, as they were taken by apparatus capable of being carried by an officer in the Field, the negatives being on Eastman's paper.' The photographs mostly show people and scenery, although there is one picture of a mountain battery in action. This group, taken at the Medical Mess at Mandalay, consists of the medical officers attached to No. 5 British and Nos. 14 and 20 Native Field Hospitals. 'There are a large number of Medical officers in Burmah, but not more than are needed; the Hospitals are full to overflowing, and in spite of large batches of sick sent down, very frequently to the base Hospital at Rangoon, the numbers still increase. The wounded are comparatively few, most cases being due to the ill-effects of climate.'

Mountain Battery ready for Action

North-West Frontier Wars 1890

Photographer unknown
Copyright : National Army Museum

In the early nineteenth century it became evident that a way had to be found to transport artillery through mountainous or jungle country, impassable to wheeled vehicles. The first mountain battery was founded in 1851, and its importance grew as activity on the North-West Frontier of India increased. The guns were made so that they could be dismantled into loads of suitable weights which could then be carried by mules. A series of photographs taken about 1903, in the possession of the Army Museum, show a 10-pounder, breech-loading, jointed mountain gun broken down into six loads for carriage by mule.

Colonel Graham, in his album on the British expeditionary force to Mandalay and Upper Burma in 1886–7, gives a description of the mountain batteries in that campaign: 'Each Battery consists of six guns – the gunners are from the Royal Artillery, the drivers being natives of India. . . . These Batteries, armed with screw guns, were first introduced at the commencement of the Afghan war, in which they did excellent service, being engaged not only in Cabul, but also at Kandahar, and also in the memorable march from Cabul to Kandahar.'

Maxim Gun detachment, 1st Battalion King's Royal Rifles

North-West Frontier Wars Chitral Relief Expedition 1895

Photographer unknown
Copyright : National Army Museum

Wars on the North-West Frontier arose out of Britain's fears that the expansion of Russia into central Asia would threaten her position in India. Between the Punjab and Afghanistan lay a large area inhabited by independent Pathan tribes. A new frontier dividing Afghanistan and India was agreed on in 1893. Serious fighting took place while the British were trying to extend their influence in Chitral in 1895, when

there were local disturbances over the disputed succession to the throne. The British Resident was besieged in Chitral Fort from 3 March until 19 April 1895, and the relief force sent to his aid had a hard march through difficult country: 'Gun and carriage loads each weighed 200 lb, and each ammunition box 125 lb. The heat in the sun was great and the glare intense.' The men had to march through the mountains practically without transport, and to negotiate a pass 12,000 feet high.

The first machine guns used by the British Army were the American Gatling guns, introduced around 1871. The first automatic machine gun, the Maxim, was introduced in 1888, and the gun in the photograph is probably the 1893 Calibre ·45, as the new 1895 Calibre ·303 was likely not to have reached India in time for this action.

N.C.O.s of The Head-quarters, Suakin Field Force

Sudanese Wars 1881–98
1885

Photograph by the Royal Engineers' Photographic Team
Copyright : Institution of Royal Engineers

The Sudanese, who had long suffered under Egyptian misrule, in 1881 revolted under the leadership of Mohammed Ahmed, known as the Mahdi. The British were drawn into the conflict through their loose protectorate over Egypt. The Battles of El Teb and Tamai were fought outside Suakin in 1884, the British force under Sir Gerald Graham defeating the Dervish followers of the Mahdi. Suakin was a port on the Red Sea and the British base. The 10th Company of the Royal Engineers, to which the photographic team was attached, did not arrive in Suakin until most of the action was over. Their function was the same as it had been in Abyssinia under Sergeant Harrold, and was primarily to record installations, fortifications and general terrain for the War Office and for map-making. The Headquarters of the Suakin Field Force to which this group of NCOs who are photographed belonged, probably contained clerks from most units at the Suakin base. The group here includes two Royal Engineers NCOs and two Royal Navy ratings. The 10th (Railway) Company of the Royal Engineers had been sent out to assist Lucas and Aird in the construction of the Suakin to Berber Railway, but the project was discontinued after only eighteen miles had been constructed. The photographic team had been trained at the School of Military Engineering, Chatham, and were only attached to the 10th Company for administrative purposes.

In January Gordon had been killed at Khartoum, and later on in the month Graham's forces had suffered heavy casualties near Suakin through an attack by Osman Digna. The British government had been wavering about the correct action to take, and when a threat of trouble with Russia over Afghanistan blew up it provided Gladstone with the excuse to withdraw British troops from the Sudan, leaving the Mahdists in control for the next thirteen years.

Camerons and Seaforths burying their dead after The Battle of Atbara

Sudanese Wars 1881–98
8 April 1898

Photograph attributed to Lieutenant the Hon.
E.D. Loch, Grenadier Guards
Copyright : National Army Museum

The photographer responsible for this next group of pictures of the Sudan was probably Lieutenant the Hon. E.D. Loch of the 1st Battalion, Grenadier Guards. Another possibility is that Francis Gregson, a friend of *The Times* correspondent, H. Howard, may have taken them. The photographer, whoever he was, must have been an amateur attached to the 1st Battalion and Loch was certainly responsible for distributing the photographs afterwards. They are informal, lively pictures and include one of Kitchener on the battlefield of Omdurman, and another, too indistinct to be shown here, of a Dervish attack.

The failure to save Gordon had rankled in Britain, and this, coupled with fears of growing French and Italian influence in Africa, led to a new campaign in 1896, when 15,000 British and Egyptian troops under General (later Lord) Kitchener invaded the Sudan. Kitchener advanced slowly, taking Dongola on 21 September and Abu Hamed on 7 August 1897. The following spring the expedition reached Atbara, where a large force of Dervishes was waiting for them. After a preliminary bombardment, the British advanced with the Cameron Highlanders in front, followed closely by the Seaforth Highlanders, the Lincolnshire and Warwickshire Regiments and Sudanese regiments. With the pipes playing and cries of 'Remember Gordon', the Dervishes were defeated. The Highlanders lost three officers and eighteen men.

Kitchener leaving the battlefield of Omdurman with his own flag and The Khalifa's Black Banner

Sudanese Wars 1881–98
2 September 1898, 11.30 a.m.

Photograph attributed to Lieutenant the Hon. E.D. Loch, Grenadier Guards
Copyright : Royal Commonwealth Society

Kitchener's forces reached Omdurman, near Khartoum, in August 1898. The Mahdists had made it their capital. As the correspondent of the *Illustrated London News* said (September 1898), 'Gordon was the real founder of Omdurman, which he found a village fifteen years ago, and himself fortified against the Mahdi. After its fall, the Dervishes centred there, and the straw and mud houses increased by thousands.' With 26,000 troops, one-third of whom were British, Kitchener attacked on 2 September. In spite of a superiority of numbers, the Mahdists were beaten, losing 11,000 men to the British forty-eight. Kitchener then marched on to the town, bringing with him the Khalifa's black flag, which had been found on the battlefield. 'Round it,' noticed an eyewitness, 'lay a mass of white-clad bodies, in appearance forming what might have been likened to a large white croquet ground or lawn tennis court outlined on the yellow sand.' Kitchener provoked much opposition in Britain by the destruction of the Mahdi's tomb at Omdurman and by his macabre treatment of the Mahdi's skull. First he considered the idea of using it as an inkwell, and then suggested that it should be sent to the College of Surgeons in London. Queen Victoria expressed her disapproval and the remains of the Mahdi were buried at Wadi Haifa. The Battle of Omdurman completed the reconquest of the Sudan and in January 1899 Britain and Egypt established a condominium later called Anglo-Egyptian Sudan.

Looting after The Battle of Omdurman

Sudanese Wars 1881–98
2 September 1898

Photograph attributed to Lieutenant the Hon.
E. D. Loch, Grenadier Guards
Copyright : National Army Museum

Colonel Villiers Hatton, commander of the 1st Battalion, Grenadier Guards, kept a diary of the advance on Khartoum, and gives this description of the battlefield of Omdurman at the end of the day: 'Officers from all regiments had been sent out to count the dead on the battlefield. G. Legh was in command. Strong escorts were taken, and the ground was divided into sections. The number – twice counted – was declared to be 10,800, of which 5,000 were of the Dervish first attack. . . . It appears that the native soldiery had shown so keen an appreciation of the loot to be found at Omdurman that the night before most articles of value had been appropriated by them, and the only way for the British to get anything interesting was to buy it from the blacks.'

The Dervishes had attempted to overwhelm the British at Omdurman by charging them in force, armed with spears and knives, but these tactics were suicidal against an enemy waiting for them armed with rifles and machine-guns.

The Back of Gordon's Palace, Khartoum

Sudanese Wars 1881–98
September 1898

Photograph attributed to Lieutenant the Hon.
E. D. Loch, Grenadier Guards
Copyright: National Army Museum

After the Battle of Omdurman the British
entered Khartoum again, thirteen years after
Gordon's death, and the troops were interested
sightseers among the ruins of Gordon's Palace.
The *Illustrated London News* describes the fight
for the town: 'Here the Dervishes, foot and
horse, made desperate charges, but in vain . . .
and while the Cavalry cut off the retreat of the
enemy to Omdurman, a pursuit was
commenced, driving the fugitives away into the
desert' (10 September). Some weeks later a
memorial service was held for Gordon which

was particularly poignant for those who had
been with the unsuccessful relief force in 1885:
'The ceremony was of the most impressive
character. . . . On Gordon's ruined palace the
flags of the Queen and the Khedive were
displayed simultaneously, while the bands
played the British and Egyptian anthems, and
the gun-boats thundered a salute' (*Illustrated
London News*, 1 October 1898).

   Colonel Villiers Hatton noted in his diary
that 'representatives of all ranks from all
regiments went up the river in gunboats to
attend a memorial service to Gordon at
Government House, Khartoum. . . . At the end
we were all allowed half an hour to stroll
around in Khartoum. . . . Everyone took
something away with him as a memento.
Banfield, my orderly, got a piece of the stone
from the steps where Gordon was murdered,
and I got a piece of elder from the garden,
which was afterwards made into a good stick.'

123

Mess Line, Tampa

Spanish-American War 1898
c. May 1898

Photographer unknown
Copyright : National Archives, Washington DC

Public opinion in America had been excited by the Cuban revolt against the Spanish in 1895. One of the more sensational newspapers cried 'Blood on the doorsteps'. In February 1898 the American battleship *Maine* arrived in Havana on a friendly visit and blew up, killing 260 officers and men. The cause of the explosion was not determined, but President McKinley, yielding to popular feeling, recognized Cuban independence, and on 25 April war was declared. Volunteers for the Army poured in and some were sent to Tampa in Florida, which had been selected by the Government as the port best suited for embarkation to Cuba. Writing from Tampa to *Harper's Weekly*, 4 June 1898, Poultney Bigelow reported on the general incompetence of Army organization: 'Here we are 30 days after the declaration of war and not a regiment is yet equipped with uniforms suitable for hot weather.' This photograph shows the troops unsuitably dressed in 'cowhide boots, thick flannel shirts, and winter trousers', waiting for their rations. Of the latter Bigelow said: 'In this hot climate we yearn for fresh fruit and vegetables, for anything that will quench thirst and at the same time cool the blood. Meat and all heating things we try to avoid by a wise instinct. The troops, however, are supplied with only that which is most unseasonable – greasy pork, and beans of that brown quality that makes one ready to spend the rest of the day in the watermelon-patch.' The invasion force left for Cuba, and a tropical climate, on 14 June still clad in their heavy winter clothes.

Men climbing on to the Dock at Daiquiri

Spanish-American War 1898
c. 22 June 1898

Photographer unknown
Copyright : National Archives, Washington DC

It was decided to make two landings on Cuba, one at Daiquiri, fifteen miles east of Santiago and the other at Siboney close by. The photograph, which may have been taken by James Burton of *Harper's Weekly*, shows the confused scene at the pier, which had been constructed a few years back by an American iron-ore company. A naval man secures the boat while the landing-party scrambles out. The landing was unopposed, although the beach could have easily been defended. Linares, the Spanish commander, chose instead to fight inland on the approach to Santiago. An eye-witness, Richard Harding Davis, described the landing at Daiquiri: 'Under the cover of the smoke the long-boats and launches began to scurry toward the shore. . . . The men in the boats pulled harder at the oars, the steam-launches rolled and pitched, tugging at the weight behind (as they towed the lines of boats), and the first convoy of five hundred men were soon bunched together, racing bow by bow for the shore. A launch turned suddenly and steered for a long pier under the ore-docks, the waves lifted it to the level of the pier, and a half-dozen men leaped through the air and landed on the pier-head, waving their muskets above them. At the same moment two of the other boats were driven through the surf to the beach itself, and the men tumbled out and scrambled to their feet upon the shore of Cuba.'

9th Infantry disembarking at Siboney

Spanish-American War   1898
25 June 1898

Photograph by Lieutenant Wise
Copyright : National Archives, Washington DC

From 25 June Siboney became the main American base for the attack on Santiago, and the troops from the first landings gathered there to meet the new arrivals. Landing was more difficult, as there was no pier, and the men were dumped out into the surf and waded for the shore. A member of the American Expeditionary Force, Lieutenant Wise, took the photograph as the boats approached the beach. The captains in charge of the transport ships were nervous of the possibility of Spanish gunfire and stayed well back. Some of the ships can be seen in the background of the photograph. Richard Harding Davis, observing the scene, said: 'Soon the sea was dotted with

rows of white boats filled with men bound about with white blanket-rolls and with muskets at all angles, and as they rose and fell on the water . . . the scene was strangely suggestive of a boat-race, and one almost waited for the starting gun.' The landings at Siboney went on until late on the night of 25 June: 'No one slept that night, for until two o'clock in the morning troops were still being disembarked in the surf, and two ships of war had their searchlights turned on the landing-place, and made Siboney as light as a ballroom. Back of the searchlights was an ocean white with moonlight, and on the shore red camp-fires, at which the half-drowned troops were drying their uniforms, and the Rough Riders, who had just marched in from Daiquiri, were cooking their coffee and bacon. . . . It was one of the most weird and remarkable scenes of the war, probably of any war. An army was being landed on an enemy's coast at the dead of night, but with somewhat more of cheers and shrieks and laughter than rise from the bathers in the surf at Coney Island on a hot Sunday.'

American troops at Daiquiri

Spanish-American War 1898
c. 24 June 1898

Photograph by William Dinwiddie
Copyright : Library of Congress, Washington DC

This interesting photograph by William Dinwiddie, who later became *Harper's* chief correspondent on Cuban affairs, clearly shows the tropical country in which the Americans had to fight. Running across the foreground of the picture is the railway, used by the American iron-ore company, and now sabotaged by the Spanish before they retreated. On the day of the first landings at Daiquiri the correspondent of the Chicago *Record*, Kennett F. Harris, had written: 'A little later with Capt O'Neill, I climbed the hill to the still smoking ruins of the roundhouse that the Spanish had burned before evacuating the town. There were a few charred timbers still standing over the mass of twisted bolts, shafts and plates that had been a locomotive.' Not only was the railway line unusable, but too few horses had been brought, and many were unfit for service after the sea journey and a swim ashore in rough water. Generally the American Government had made inadequate preparations for the war in Cuba. The troops were still in their heavy uniforms, rations were inadequate and medical arrangements poor. As a *Harper's* correspondent said: 'They fought in an unknown country, amid strange surroundings, tortured by tropical insects and tropical vegetation, soaked by tropical rains, and breathing pestilential air while they slept.' (July 16 1898) In the photograph the Expeditionary Force are marching towards the hills occupied by the Spanish, behind the beach-head. Linares had chosen to fight at Las Guasimas, a gap in the hills guarding the approach to Santiago.

watching attack on Caney

Watching the attack on El Caney

Spanish-American War   1898
1 July 1898

Photographer unknown
Copyright : National Archives, Washington DC

After a successful attack on Las Guasimas on June 24 the American troops could see Santiago, but the hills in front of the city were held by the Spanish. General Shafter's main attack was directed against San Juan Hill, and the secondary assault was on El Caney, a small village to the north-east. General Lawton's division attacked on 1 July, finally pushing back the 520 Spanish troops under General del Rey. General Shafter assigned four guns to reduce the defences at El Caney and two others to bombard San Juan Hill. The guns, seen here in the photograph, were later described by an artillery officer, Dwight E. Aultman. They were

3·2 field guns, 'the latest and last development of the old non-recoil material, firing unfixed ammunition with black powder charges and unprovided with any of the laying apparatus for indirect fire'. By this time the French 75 mm gun had been developed 'with its fixed ammunition, rapid fire and indirect laying. Yet such was our backwardness in military science that the whole Army was ignorant of the tremendous advance in Field Artillery that in 1898 was an accomplished fact.' Another eye-witness saw 'the four guns unlimbered and thrown into position against Caney, the caissons drawn to the rear, the horses gathered into the bushes to one side, and officers, aides, and correspondents walked the length of the hill, or stood in groups watching with field-glasses the red town, the stone fort to the right, and the block-house to the right of it. . . .' The battle took much longer than Lawton had reckoned with, and his force was too late to help with the San Juan attack. The Spanish commander was killed in the last moments of the fighting.

Ambulance at the foot of San Juan Hill

Spanish-American War   1898
1 July 1898

Photograph by A.D. Brittingham
Copyright : National Archives, Washington DC

Writing about the Battle of San Juan, Richard Harding Davis said: 'I have seen many illustrations and pictures of this charge on the San Juan hills, but none of them seem to show it just as I remember it. In the picture-papers the men are running up-hill swiftly and gallantly, in regular formation, rank after rank, with flags flying, their eyes aflame, and their hair streaming, their bayonets fixed, in long, brilliant lines, an invincible, overpowering weight of numbers. Instead of which I think the thing which impressed one the most, when our men started from cover, was that they were so few. It seemed as if someone had made an awful and terrible mistake. One's instinct was to

call to them to come back.' Stephen Crane sent a dispatch to *Harper's* describing the wounded 'stringing back from the front, hundreds of them. . . . And then there were the slow-pacing stretcher-bearers, with the dying or insensible. . . . Everywhere moved the sure-handed, invaluable Red Cross men.' There was a field hospital in a clearing near the River Aguadores. The Regimental Surgeon of the 3rd Cavalry, George J. Newgarden, working there, said: 'The wounded came pouring in from over the bank in a steady stream, some limping, some hopping, others holding their arms to their sides or abdomen, many using the rifle as a crutch or support, and a number carried in by their comrades. . . . The capacity of the dressing-station was very soon strained to its utmost.' Casualties were very heavy and the Americans with difficulty maintained their foothold on the ridges overlooking Santiago. Gradually trenches were dug and the positions strengthened, and the battle settled down into a state of siege.

Raising the American flag on The Casa Municipal, Santiago

Spanish-American War   1898
17 July 1898

Photographer unknown
Copyright : National Archives, Washington DC

The American bombardment and the naval blockade forced Santiago to capitulate on Sunday, 17 July 1898. General Wheeler announced the Spanish surrender at Church Parade on San Juan Hill. He then marched with General Shafter and a small force into Santiago. The townspeople gathered in the main square to watch the American flag being raised over the Governor's Palace as the clock struck twelve. 'At the same moment 21 guns were fired and the band of the 6th Cavalry

struck up "Hail, Columbia". The 9th Infantry, which was drawn up in the plaza, presented arms to the American colors' (General Wheeler's account). Lieutenant C.D. Rhodes described in his diary the antics of a war correspondent called Sylvester Scovel, who represented the New York *World*. Anxious to obtain a scoop, he 'insisted in mounting to the roof of the Governor's Palace where the flag raising was to take place, but much to his indignation was ordered down by Colonel Miley, in charge of the ceremony. Thereupon Scovel appealed to General Shafter in a loud voice, while the General and his staff were standing before the assembled troops. . . . Some words followed, and I saw Scovel strike or attempt to strike General Shafter in the face. Scovel was hustled off by the soldiers and the ceremony proceeded.' A more law-abiding photographer can be seen on the left of the picture recording the scene.

The Mounted Leicesters reaching Ladysmith from Dundee

2nd Boer War   1899–1902
October 1899

Photograph by Horace W. Nicholls
Copyright : Royal Photographic Society

The success enjoyed by her Army in the minor conflicts of the nineteenth century, most of them against native troops, left Britain unprepared for the setbacks of the Boer War.

At the height of the war Britain had 250,000 men in the field compared with a Boer force that never exceeded 60,000 but still could not be subdued. Hostilities commenced in October 1899, when the Boers under Joubert advanced into Natal, aiming to capture the port of Durban, while another force under Cronje made towards Mafeking and Kimberley in the west. The Boer army advancing into Natal was well-armed and superior in numbers to the British force under the command of General Sir George White. They reached Dundee, a small coal-mining village 120 miles from Durban, on 20 October, and drove back the British at the

Battle of Talana Hill. The following day there were heavy casualties on both sides at Elandslaagte. The British, fighting a rearguard action, were steadily squeezed back to Ladysmith.

A Johannesburg photographer, Horace Nicholls, took a series of remarkably fine photographs of the British retreat to Ladysmith. Apart from sending his pictures to illustrated journals, he also published a series of exhibition prints 'printed in Permanent Carbon', and costing £1 1s. for an 18″ × 11″ print. The cavalrymen photographed here look exhausted and one trooper on the right of the picture has

fallen asleep in the saddle. In the catalogue of his photographs, Nicholls wrote: 'In introducing this Series of Carbons to the public, I should say that having so frequently heard the remark in criticism of the fine pictures (representing War Scenes) produced by our best artists, "Oh yes, it's a grand piece of work, but it is only the artist's imagination", I have made it my great aim throughout the Campaign to produce a series of large photographs which would appeal to the artistic sense of the most fastidious, knowing that they must as photographs have the enhanced value of being truthful.'

tr a Hard Day - Ladysmith (K.R.R.) *Horace W. Nicholls*

After a heavy Day—Ladysmith

2nd Boer War 1899–1902
October 1899

Photograph by Horace W. Nicholls
Copyright : Royal Photographic Society

Taken during General Yule's retreat to
Ladysmith in October 1899, this remarkable
photograph looks forward in style to some of
the 1st World War pictures, interpreting very
clearly the weariness of the King's Royal Rifles
at the end of a long day. The retreat took place
at the height of the rainy season and the troops
met with impassable mud and swollen rivers.
Unable to retreat to Ladysmith by a direct
route, General Yule made an epic march by
way of Helpmakaar and a sixty-four-mile
roundabout route to avoid the Boer army.
The Boers were in pursuit and harrassed the
rearguard. After three days and nights of

marching the Dundee detachment containing
the 1st Battalion of the King's Royal Rifles met
up with the main force and their own 2nd
Battalion. George Lynch, whose drawing of the
march was published in the *Illustrated London
News* of 25 November 1899, said: 'Some idea of
the fatigues of General Yule's forced march
from Dundee may be gathered from the pictures
of our gallant troops fording a stream knee-deep
in the water. This march, we now learn, was
made on such rough sustenance as biscuit, salt
beef, and muddy water, and many men dropped
out of the ranks dead asleep.' Commenting on
Nicholls's photographs, the *Cape Argus* said:
'The pictures of Yule's Column on its way to
Ladysmith from Dundee, are worthy of Lady
Butler or Caton Woodville, so careful has Mr
Nicholls been in his work, and so admirably has
he avoided the pitfalls into which so many of his
fellow artists fall in photographing any moving
objects.'

The Handy Man. To the Relief of Ladysmith   Horace W.

The Handy Man (to the relief of Ladysmith)

2nd Boer War   1899–1902
October 1899

Photograph by Horace W. Nicholls
Copyright : Royal Photographic Society

Yule's army arrived in Ladysmith on 24
October. At the same time a contingent of naval
gunners from HMS *Powerful* with 12-pdr. guns
was advancing from Durban, and they arrived
at Ladysmith shortly before the Boers completed their encircling manœuvre. Although a
shell from the Boer guns on Petworth Hill,
north of the town, burst beside one of their
guns and overturned it, they were able to
silence the powerful 'Long Tom' gun of the
Boers. These naval-ship guns were adapted for
use on land by a special carriage designed by
Captain Percy Scott. Nicholls has photographed
a detachment of the Naval Brigade, with their
characteristic flat hats, advancing to the relief of
Ladysmith. In the catalogue of his exhibition
prints, the following comment is made about
this picture: 'The surrounding scenery in this
picture has more variety in it than any other of
the series, and the whole scene, including men
and guns (on their way to Ladysmith) forms a
striking and interesting picture, which delights
the artistic sense as well as quickening the
appreciation of this useful branch of Her
Majesty's service.' The naval blue-jacket
brigade, nicknamed the 'Handy Man' by
contemporaries, 'came upon dejected
Ladysmith like a sea breeze straying among
worn-out dwellers inland', as the correspondent
of the *Illustrated London News* picturesquely
put it.

Ladysmith, after Nicholson's Nek

2nd Boer War 1899–1902
30 October 1899

Photograph by Horace W. Nicholls
Copyright: Royal Photographic Society

Two actions were fought outside Ladysmith on 29 and 30 October to prevent the town from being encircled by the Boer army. These were at Nicholson's Nek and Farquhars Farm. Although the arrival of the naval guns provided some respite for the hardly-pressed troops, the British finally had to retreat hurriedly into the town. General Joubert was later criticized for not pursuing the retreating army. There was panic inside Ladysmith, as an eyewitness reported: 'The condition of the women, wan and weary with waiting, was pitiable in the extreme. The barbarity of war was more marked in the horror written on those pale faces . . . than in the mangled frames borne from the battlefield.' Nicholls's catalogue of *Historic Pictures* describes this photograph as being 'one of the gems of the collection, and apart from its historical interest, is a veritable triumph of photography. The ox wagons and mule wagons, laden with war material, drawn aside to make way for the troops coming in through the dust from the field, are such good effect that one doubts if this be not after all a carefully planned composition.' The mule wagons, with equipment for four days' fighting, had been waiting in the street for over twelve hours in the hope of a British advance. After 119 days of siege, Ladysmith was finally relieved by General Buller's army on 28 February 1900.

Men of The Dublin Fusiliers mounting the armoured train at Estcourt

2nd Boer War   1899–1902
15 November 1899

Photograph by Horace W. Nicholls
Copyright : Royal Photographic Society

The railways played an important part in Boer War strategy. Ladysmith stood at the junction of two lines which ran from Natal into both Boer republics. Estcourt, on the railway line south from Ladysmith, became a military base, and on 15 November an armoured train was sent up the line on a reconnaissance patrol. The train consisted of a central engine and tender with two trucks on one side and three on the other. The sides of the trucks were covered in steel plating with loopholes through which the soldiers could fire. Patrols on this train were unpopular with the soldiers, as the line could easily be ambushed by Boer commandos. One survivor recalls: 'How relieved the occupants looked when they climbed over its plated sides and congratulated themselves that their turn to form the freight of this moribund engine of war would not come round again for at least some days.' The Dublin Fusiliers staffed the patrol on 15 November, and among the civilians on board was Winston Churchill, newly arrived in Estcourt as correspondent for the *Morning Post*. One of his colleagues of the Press was Rene Bull of *Black and White*. When the train reached Chievely, fourteen miles up the line, the Boers were waiting. Their guns opened fire, the train was wrecked and after a spirited defence fifty-six British troops and Churchill were taken prisoner. The engine was saved, due partly to Churchill's efforts, and returned to Estcourt with forty wounded. The survivors were full of praise for Churchill's part in the action, and the newspapers made much of the incident. A story of personal bravery was always good propaganda and an antidote to the gloomy stories of British defeats on other fronts, and a suitable climax to the tale was Churchill's escape on 26 December.

Watching The Battle of Colenso
2nd Boer War   1899–1902
15 December 1899

Photograph by David Barnett
Copyright: National Army Museum

When David Barnett's photograph was on display in London in 1900, a critic said: 'The war pictures that take the most prominent position for the fine quality are those taken by Mr D. Barnett of Johannesburg. . . . Action is portrayed here by the camera that once and for all stamps it as the perfect instrument in the hands of the artist.' (*Amateur Photographer*, 16 February 1900) *Black and White* published the photograph, acknowledging it to 'Rene Bull and D. Barnett'. Once again Bull had been quick to claim credit for other people's photographs. The usual difficulties of taking photographs under battle conditions were added to at Colenso by dust and haze, described by another photographer, W.K.L. Dickson, who was present at the battle on behalf of Biograph Films. Dickson had to abandon his camera on one occasion during the day when a Boer shell hit the British Red Cross wagons and

he helped to carry away the wounded. A Colonel who saw him remarked: 'This is hardly Biographing.'

Colenso was one of the battles of the Tugela River which Buller's troops had to cross to reach besieged Ladysmith. A two-day bombardment by the 1st Brigade Division of the Royal Field Artillery was to precede the attack. The 14th and 66th Batteries made up this Division, and were under the personal supervision of the CRA Natal, Colonel C.J. Long. They had six naval 12-pdr. guns drawn by oxen. The photograph shows the reserve force with a 45-pdr. The two sides were only four miles apart, and the British looked down towards the Boers, who had dug in along the hills lining the north bank of the Tugela, overlooking the village of Colenso. Soon after the photograph was taken, Colonel Long took the guns further forward in an attempt to silence the Boer artillery and facilitate the British infantry's river crossing. He advanced too far and in the confusion which followed Buller ordered the Artillery back and ten guns were lost. The action was a personal disaster for General Buller. Louis telegraphed the Volksraad: 'Today the God of our fathers has given us a great victory.'

The British Gun 'Joe Chamberlain' firing lyddite shell on The Kopjes of Magersfontein
2nd Boer War   1899–1902
10–11 December 1899

Photograph by Reinhold Thiele
Copyright : Radio Times Hulton Picture Library

Lord Methuen was in charge of the Kimberley Relief Force. After fighting at Belmont, Enslin and the Modder River, Methuen had lost 10 per cent of his original army, but some reinforcements had arrived in time for the action at Magersfontein on 10–11 December 1899. Thiele's photograph shows the naval 4·7″ gun 'Joe Chamberlain' firing at the Boer trenches in the Magersfontein hills. G Battery of the RHA manned the gun and Lieutenant Campbell (on the right) was in command. The gun is in a pit dug in the open veldt, without any embrasure. In the barrage which preceded the attack, an onlooker wrote: 'The hail of shrapnel and the great volcano jets of red earth and ironstone boulders hurled fifty feet by the bursting lyddite, seemed to convert the whole hillside into a perfect inferno of fire.' Unfortunately, the bombardment had little effect, as the Boers had dug in deeply. Only their morale was rather shaken as they did not agree with bombardments being on a Sunday. The British attack, when it came, was a failure, heavy losses were suffered and the army withdrew to the Modder River. Combined with British defeats on other fronts at Stormberg and Colenso, the week of 10–17 December 1899 became known as the 'black week'.

When Thiele's photograph was finally published in the *Graphic* in March 1900 there was no indication in the caption that the action at Magersfontein had not been successful.

Arrival of the Christmas mail at De Aar

2nd Boer War   1899–1902
Christmas 1899

Photograph by Reinhold Thiele
Copyright : Radio Times Hulton Picture Library

Reinhold Thiele was a German Press
photographer, resident in London, who had
been commissioned by the *Graphic* to cover the
Boer War, and joined Lord Methuen's force
advancing towards the relief of Kimberley.
After the defeat at Magersfontein and the
retreat to the Modder there was little action to
photograph. H.C. Shelley, another
photographer with Methuen, described in the
Amateur Photographer his boredom with life at
the Modder River station when he could only
take pictures of camp life for two months.
Thiele made use of the time, and later, on his
return from the war, published exhibition
prints of 611 subjects taken with his $10'' \times 8''$
plate camera.

De Aar was an important railway junction
controlling the route to the Cape, some
distance south of the Modder River station. It
became a military base for the advance on the
enemy capitals of Bloemfontein and Pretoria.
The *Graphic* captioned a similar photograph
taken by Thiele: 'The arrival of the Christmas
mail was eagerly looked for by men of Lord
Methuen's force. When it arrived the sorting at
the military Post Office was a sad task. There
were so many letters for men who had fallen in
battle.'

The Battlefield: Spion Kop

2nd Boer War   1899–1902
January 1900

Unknown Boer photographer
Copyright : Radio Times Hulton Picture Library

The Boers used this photograph as propaganda to encourage their troops with the sight of British casualties. The reaction of the *Amateur Photographer* (2 August 1901) is typical of the British response: 'The recently published photographs depicting the carnage among our troops at the Battle of Spion Kop, fought on 24 and 25 January 1900, and one taken ten days afterwards, depicting the unburied dead, can serve no useful purpose, and appeals to the morbid side of human nature solely.' The photograph is unusual in one respect: The Boers usually replaced their clothing by stripping dead British soldiers, as well as prisoners-of-war.

The action at Spion Kop formed part of General Buller's campaign to relieve Ladysmith. General Warren hoped that by taking Spion Kop, the highest feature of a ridge of hills guarding the route from Trickhardt's Drift to Ladysmith, he would gain a commanding position. The hill became a death-trap for the British, who were only able to dig shallow trenches and were under fire from all sides. Deneys Reitz, who was with the Boer commandos, says: 'There cannot have been many battlefields where there was such an accumulation of horrors within so small a compass. . . . In the shallow trenches where they had fought the soldiers lay dead in swathes, and in places they were piled three deep.' British casualties totalled 1,200. Botha granted a twenty-four-hour truce for the wounded to be removed and the dead buried.

The news of the disaster in England brought criticism of the Government and shock at the number of casualties. However, the ill-omened name of Spion Kop did not dismay one enterprising British manufacturer, who brought out a 'Spion Kop Camera', a magazine-type box camera with six metal slides for 30s. As Spion Kop would remain in everyone's memories, so he hoped would his camera be remembered and purchased. His advertising brainwave was considered to be in rather bad taste.

Officers' Mess, 3rd Grenadiers on the Modder

2nd Boer War 1899–1902
February 1900

Photograph by Reinhold Thiele
Copyright: Radio Times Hulton Picture Library

This photograph was published in the *Graphic* on 10 March 1900 with the caption: 'It is difficult to recognize the smart Grenadiers when paraded in their campaigning kit.' The unit was under the command of Colonel E.M.S. Crabbe, 'who is well-known to Londoners in connection with the Military Tournament'. Khaki, used first for service on the Indian frontier, was adopted for regular use in the Boer War. Deneys Reitz, when first in action with the Boer commandos, was disappointed to see that 'Officers and men were dressed in drab khaki uniforms, instead of the scarlet I had seen in England'. But in the earlier stages of the war the camouflaging qualities of khaki were spoilt by the use of white equipment and helmets. Later on a number of units started to wear slouch hats similar to those worn by the Boers, which sometimes led to cases of mistaken identity.

In spite of Cardwell's reforms in the 1860s, there were still many deficiencies in the British Army, both in leadership and training, which soon became apparent after the defeats of the 'Black Week' of December 1899. At the beginning of the war Buller had been confident of a quick victory. After the 'Black Week' the mood changed completely. Control passed from Buller to Roberts and Kitchener. There was a rush of volunteers, and 8,000 mounted troops were raised which were called the Imperial Yeomanry. The most famous of the unmounted volunteers were the City Imperial Volunteers. The majority of volunteers came from the upper classes.

The Grenadiers were with Lord Methuen's force advancing to the relief of Kimberley. They were in action on the Modder in November 1899, and suffered heavy casualties at Belmont on 23 November. In February 1900, when the photograph was taken, they were at Modder River Camp prior to the engagement which led to the surrender of Cronje on 18 February.

144

Crossing the Modder River

2nd Boer War   1899–1902
February 1900

Photograph by Captain Holson, RFA, *and*
Reinhold Thiele
Copyright : Radio Times Hulton Picture Library

Methuen's troops remained inactive at the
Modder River station for two months after
their defeat at Magersfontein on 10–11
December 1899. An editorial in the *Illustrated
London News* on 10 February 1900 says with
some asperity: 'At Modder River the very
provoking state of inaction continues, but there
are signs that it will shortly be brought to a
close. . . . It is no doubt satisfactory to learn
that in the meantime the troops at Modder
River have been wholesomely engaged in a
series of inter-regimental boxing-matches; but
it will have occurred forcibly to most of us that
this is scarcely the *"raison d'être"* of their
presence in that quarter.' At the end of 1899
control of military operations passed to Lord
Roberts, with Kitchener as his second-in-
command. Roberts reached Cape Town on 10
January, where he received a message from
Cecil Rhodes in besieged Kimberley: 'There is
no fear our surrendering, but we are getting
anxious about the state of the British Army. It
is high time you did something.' Roberts stirred
Methuen's static troops into action and the
advance commenced on 11 February, led by
General French's cavalry division. Two rivers,
the Riet and Modder, lay between them and
Kimberley. The Modder was reached on
13 February.

According to an album in possession of the
Army Museum, Captain Holson, 82nd Battery,
RFA, took this photograph, which was later
copied and circulated by Thiele. The Royal
Canadian Regiment are seen crossing
Paardeberg Drift just behind the 82nd Battery
RFA. The photographic plates made here were
almost certainly sent home for processing. Mud
from the Modder River was a particular
problem for photographers. Any water used had
to be allowed to stand for several hours so that
the mud would settle, but even then the
negatives had a sandpapery surface.

Canadians seizing a kopje: The Toronto Company's baptism of fire

2nd Boer War   1899–1902
February 1900

*Photograph by Captain Holson, RFA, and
Reinhold Thiele*
Copyright : National Army Museum

General French's division marched into Kimberley on 15 February. Cronje retreated eastwards to Paardeberg, twenty-three miles away on the Modder River. Here he was cornered by Kitchener's forces on 18 February. The Canadians and the 82nd RFA were in action together on Gun Hill, and Captain Holson's photograph shows C Company of the Royal Canadian Regiment under Captain Barker storming a kopje. The picture clearly shows the rough ground, where the advancing troops had to get what shelter they could behind the boulders. Officers generally tried to look as much like privates as possible to avoid attention from Boer snipers, and wore no badges of rank. The soldiers were armed with Lee Enfield rifles, which came into use in 1895 and continued to be issued in a modified form throughout the 1st World War and part of the 2nd. There were more British casualties at Paardeberg than on any other occasion during the war, and some blame was attached to Kitchener, who wrote later: 'I hope the authorities will keep their hair on, and if they want a victim to sacrifice I am always at their disposal. War means risks, and you cannot play the game and always win.' A British bombardment finally forced Cronje to surrender.

Field hospital at Paardeberg Drift

2nd Boer War   1899–1902
February 1900

Photograph by Reinhold Thiele
Copyright : Radio Times Hulton Picture Library

The British victory at Paardeberg led to the relief of Kimberley, which had been under siege since October 1899. Some of the many British casualties can be seen here at the Paardeberg field hospital waiting to have their wounds dressed. The Highlanders, who had played a prominent part in the attack, are among the soldiers. At this time Highland regiments wore part khaki, with khaki aprons over their kilts to remove the contrast between the tartan and the rest of the uniform. Wounds were mostly caused by Mauser rifle bullets and by shell splinters. Many of the men have been wounded in the left arm, indicating the accuracy of the Boer sharpshooters. The procedure followed when soldiers were wounded was that first the stretcher-bearers rendered 'first aid, ticket them with a number and a rough diagnosis of the nature of the injury, and leave them to be picked up and carried to the collecting stations, which are placed out of rifle-fire but not beyond the range of artillery'. During the Boer War Indian bearers often carried the stretchers. 'At the collecting-station the wounds are examined by a medical officer, and those requiring further attention are taken to the dressing stations, which are established out of the range of the big guns.' (*Illustrated London News*, special war number) From here the wounded were taken to field hospitals and then on to base hospitals. These men would have been sent to the base hospital at Bloemfontein.

General Cronje with Lord Roberts's staff

2nd Boer War   1899–1902
27 February 1900

Photograph by Rheinhold Thiele
Copyright : Radio Times Hulton Picture Library

As the Battle of Paardeberg continued, the resistance of the Boers under Cronje was gradually worn down. They were without food, their transport animals had been destroyed and their morale was low. Describing the action, the *Illustrated London News* said: 'It is sufficient to say that, in the forlorn hope of being reinforced, Cronje continued to hold out stubbornly, and that gradually the British forces closed in, at the same time severely punishing every attempt at rescue, until the enemy's position was literally hopeless.' The Boers capitulated on 27 February and soon after 7 a.m. Cronje arrived at Lord Roberts's headquarters to surrender. Kronje, in his rough civilian clothes, was a strange contrast to the British Army officers. Thiele has photographed the Boer General with Captain Watermeyer of the Cape Town Highlanders, ADC to Lord Roberts. A drawing, based on the photograph, in which Cronje appears to be very dejected and the British officers look excessively genial and victorious, was published by the *Graphic* on 14 April. Lord Roberts was reported to have said to the Boer leader when they met: 'I am glad to see you. You made a gallant defence.' The surrender of Cronje's army was a blow from which the Boers never recovered. Many prisoners were taken and Cronje was exiled to St Helena. 27 February was a particularly ironic date for the Boer surrender, as it was the anniversary of Majuba Day. President Kruger said: 'The English have taken our Majuba Day away from us.'

Creusot's Long Tom at Mafeking
2nd Boer War   1899–1902
1899–1900

Unknown Boer photographer
Copyright : Radio Times Hulton Picture Library

Mafeking, first besieged at the same time as
Ladysmith and Kimberley, was not relieved
until May 1900. 'Long Tom' was the British
Army's name for the 94-pdr. Creusot guns used
by the Boers for siege operations. The two Boer
republics had spent large sums on munitions
before the war, and were well supplied with
guns from Krupp and Creusot. The guns were
manned by the only properly disciplined troops
in the Boer Army – men of the Staats-Artillerie
and from the Transvaal police, supplemented at
the outbreak of war by over 2,000 mercenaries.
In spite of their training, the Boer artillery's
range-finding was decidedly eccentric, which
reduced the efficiency of the bombardment at
Mafeking.

In spite of their size, the Boers managed to
transport these siege guns around the
countryside, and they appear at the sieges of
Ladysmith, Kimberley and Mafeking. There
were four 'Long Toms' at Mafeking. The Boers
had very strict ideas on the ethics of war, and
when a 'Long Tom' was first used at Mafeking
General Cronje warned Baden Powell, who was
in charge of the defence, that the terrible
weapon was about to fire. The first shell killed
one chicken. Although the gunners did become
more accurate, the siege guns were not so
effective at Mafeking as in other campaigns,
because most of the buildings were single-
storied and set in large grounds, and the blast
caused little damage. The shells used were
generally shrapnel, and were not dangerous if
people took cover in shelters and dugouts. At
first the shelling came at regular times each day.
J.E. Neilly wrote in *Besieged With B.P.*: 'At
first we got our supplies of shells much as a
patient gets his pills – at regular hours and in
fixed numbers.'

Boers in Battle. Burghers Slaags.

Van Hoepen

65

Boers manning the trenches outside Mafeking

2nd Boer War 1899–1902
1899–1900

Photograph by Van Hoeden
Copyright : Radio Times Hulton Picture Library

Although this photograph was probably specially posed, it gives a clear picture of Boer sharpshooters in action. They were protected by a shallow trench from British shell-fire, and would have been practically invisible from a distance. Life for Boers employed on sieges was fairly pleasant, as they had food and plenty of home leave. Deneys Reitz, with the Boer commandos at the Siege of Ladysmith, said: 'My brother and I settled down to a life of ease, spending our time sniping at the English outposts, or riding to the neighbouring laagers.

Camp life was a pleasant existence.' The commandos had no official uniform and were equipped with modern clip-loaded Mauser rifles. A commando consisted of an average of 100 mounted riflemen reinforced by guns.

The sharpshooters' ability was underrated at the beginning of the war. One journalist even said: 'The bucolic Dutchman has lost his ancient cunning in wielding his rifle.' In fact, every man was a superb marksman. The Boers were used to hunting and to the country, and their lack of formal military training was an advantage, particularly in guerrilla warfare. The Boer superiority in marksmanship continued throughout the war, and at Elands Rivers Poort on Smuts's march through Cape Colony, Deneys Reitz says: 'As the soldiers raised their heads to fire they were brought down, being no match for us in short-range work of this kind.'

Boer Commandos at Colesberg
2nd Boer War   1899–1902
February 1900

Photograph by David Barnett
Copyright : Radio Times Hulton Picture Library

The surrender of Cronje at Paardeberg opened the way for an all-out offensive against the Boers in the Orange Free State. On 13 March 1900 Roberts occupied Bloemfontein and the Boers made Kroonstad, 100 miles to the north, their new capital. Colesberg, where Barnett's photograph was taken, was in the south of the State. With the relief of the besieged towns and the British occupation of Pretoria in June, organized Boer resistance came to an end, but guerrilla warfare continued for nearly two more years. The Boer commandos in the photograph are armed with modern rifles. Often these were obtained from the British by raiding. Deneys Reitz recalls an occasion when he was with Smuts at Elands Rivers Poort: 'I fired my last two cartridges here, and my first thought was to run to a dead soldier and seize his rifle and bandolier.' Kitchener was forced to devise new tactics to put an end to the guerrilla warfare. He set up a system of blockhouses with barbed wire between them across the veld. Boer farmhouses were burnt so that the commandos and their families would be starved out. The British made some attempt to prevent the innocent from suffering, and instituted camps for the women and children, but these quickly became insanitary and disease killed many. Peace was not made until 1902.

The Guards Brigade at Kroonstadt
2nd Boer War 1899–1902
May 1900

Photograph by Underwood and Underwood
Copyright : Radio Times Hulton Picture Library

The Guards of General Pole-Carew's division photographed here were with Lord Roberts when he occupied Kroonstadt on 2 May 1900. The stereoscopic photographs of Underwood and Underwood were the equivalent of today's picture-postcards. They were usually sold in sets and designed to appeal to a mass audience. The pictures often look posed, compared with the news photographs taken for publication in the illustrated journals by Nicholls, Barnett and Thiele. The craze for stereoscopic pictures

lasted for at least sixty years, but had died out by 1914.

For the British the Boer War was in many ways a dress rehearsal for the 1st World War. Troops in the field now wore khaki. Weapons were much the same as they would be in 1914 and many of the same commanders would be in action again during the 1st World War. Up to the time of the Boer War very much smaller forces had been needed for local imperial conflicts, and the war showed that a better trained reserve was needed. Unlike Germany, there was no compulsory service in the British Army until 1916. Trench warfare and barbed wire were present during the Boer War, but the British commanders did not learn anything useful from their experiences to help them with the stalemate of the trenches in 1914.

Dying Tibetan Soldier

Tibet 1904
1904

Photographer unknown
Copyright : National Army Museum

Although just outside the period covered, this
photograph of a dying Tibetan soldier by a
freak of chance spans nearly forty years of
photographic history, and has much more in
common with photo-journalism of the 'thirties
than with the nineteenth century. The camera's
power to freeze the moment of death is as
effective here as it was in Robert Capa's famous
Spanish Civil War photograph. As Ken Baynes
has said: 'In newspapers, war photographs are
tied to the moment, to the news of the day and,
more often than not, to the hungry desire for
victory. . . . The passage of time leaves the best
war photographs to live on as generalized
symbols.'

Index